D1548452

GIFTED AND TALENTED TEST PREPARATION

COGAT® KINDERGARTEN

300+ Questions /
2 Full-Length Practice Tests
Level 5 / 6

Savant Test Prep™
www.SavantPrep.com

Please leave a review for this book!

Thank you for purchasing this resource.

If you would take a moment to kindly leave a
review on the website where you purchased this publication,
we would greatly appreciate it.

© 2021 SavantPrep.com. All rights reserved. No part of this book may be reproduced or distributed by any means or in any form. It may not be stored in any retrieval system or database without obtaining the prior written approval of SavantPrep.com first.

SavantPrep.com is not liable for the accuracy of this content, nor is it liable for errors or for omissions of any form. SavantPrep.com publishes all material without any kind of warranty, implied or express. SavantPrep.com is not responsible for any damage or loss that may be caused by a reader/customer relying on the information in SavantPrep.com published material. All information is subject to change without notice. This publication is not intended to replace an examination given by a testing expert or psychologist. In some instances standardized tests do not provide an accurate assessment of the test-takers' cognitive abilities. The same is true with this publication. This publication's exercises are intended to build cognitive skills and abilities, which the COGAT® is designed to measure. This publication's exercises are not actual questions from tests.

The tests listed in this publication are registered trademarks of their respective publishers. COGAT® is a registered trademark of Houghton Mifflin Harcourt™. Iowa Assessments™ is a trademark of Houghton Mifflin Harcourt™. Trademarks and registered trademarks referring to tests and test publishers are used by SavantPrep.com for nominative purposes only. Trademarks and registered trademarks referring to tests and test publishers are the property of their respective owners. SavantPrep.com is not affiliated with any of these publishers or publishers' affiliates.

Houghton Mifflin Harcourt™ does not endorse nor do they sponsor this publication. SavantPrep.com publications have not been reviewed by or approved by the aforementioned test publishers.

TABLE OF CONTENTS

INTRODUCTION

COGAT® GENERAL INFORMATION

- COGAT® stands for Cognitive Abilities Test®. It measures students' reasoning skills and problem-solving skills.
- It provides educators with an overall assessment of students' academic strengths and weaknesses.
    - The test is sometimes used together with the ITBS™ (a.k.a. Iowa Test) for this purpose.
- It is commonly used as a screener for gifted and talented programs.
    - Gifted and Talented (G&T) selection sometimes requires a teacher recommendation as well.
- At this level, the test is usually administered 1-on-1 or in a small group setting.
- A teacher (or other school associate) administers the test, reading the directions. (Computerized versions of the test are also available.)
- Please check with your school / testing site regarding its testing procedures, as these may differ.

COGAT® LEVEL 5/6 FORMAT

- Students in kindergarten take the COGAT® Level 5/6.
- The test has 118 questions.
- The test is divided into 3 main parts, each called a "Battery." Each Battery has three question types. See chart below.

VERBAL BATTERY	NON-VERBAL BATTERY	QUANTITATIVE BATTERY
Picture Analogies: 14 Questions	Figure Analogies: 14 Questions	Number Puzzles: 10 Questions
Picture Classification: 14 Questions	Figure Classification: 14 Questions	Number Series: 14 Questions
Sentence Completion: 14 Questions	Paper Folding: 10 Questions	Number Analogies: 14 Questions

- Often, schools administer one Battery per day, allowing approximately 45 minutes per Battery.
- Students have around 15 minutes to complete each question type (for example, students would have around 15 minutes to complete Picture Analogies).
- See pages 6-11 for examples and explanations of each question type.

COGAT® SCORING

- Students receive points for correct answers. Points are not deducted for incorrect answers. (Therefore, students should at least guess versus leaving a question blank.)
- In general, schools have a "cut-off" COGAT® score, which they consider together with additional criteria, for gifted & talented acceptance. This varies by school.
- This score is usually at least 98%. (However, some schools accept scores 95% or even 85%.)
- A score of 98% means that your child scored as well as, or better than, 98% of children in his/her testing group.
- COGAT® scores are available for the entire test and can be broken down by Battery.
- Depending on the school/program, such a "cut-off" score may only be required on one or two of the Batteries (and not on the test overall).
- It is essential to check with your school/program for their acceptance procedures.

(The COGAT® Practice Tests in this book can not yield these percentiles because they have not been given to a large enough group of students to produce an accurate comparison / calculation.)

HOW TO USE THIS BOOK

1. Read through the question examples and explanations (p. 6 - 11). This section is for parents.

2. Do Practice Test 1.
- Do these questions together with your child, especially if this is your child's first exposure to COGAT®-prep questions.
    - Talk about what the question is asking your child to do.
- Questions progress in difficulty.
    - The first few questions are quite simple.
- Do at least one section (Verbal / Non-Verbal/ Quantitative) per day.
- Do not assign a time limit.
- Go over the answers using the Answer Key (p. 106).
    - For questions missed, go over the answers again, discussing what makes the correct answer better than the other choices.

3. Do Practice Test 2.
- If your child progressed easily through Practice Test 1, then see how well your child can do on Practice Test 2 without your help. (You will still read the directions to your child.)
- If your child needed assistance with much of Practice Test 1, then continue to assist your child with Practice Test 2.
- Do at least one section (Verbal / Non-Verbal/ Quantitative) per day.
- If you wish to assign a time limit, assign around 15 minutes per question type.
- Go over the answers using the Answer Key (p. 107).
    - For questions missed, go over the answers again, discussing what makes the correct answer better than the other choices.

4. Go to our website, www.SavantPrep.com, for FREE 10 bonus practice questions (PDF format).

> GET FREE 10 BONUS PRACTICE QUESTIONS (PDF)!
> GO TO WWW.SAVANTPREP.COM AND GET THEM TODAY.

TEST-TAKING TIPS

- Ensure your child listens carefully to the directions, especially in the Sentence Completion section.
- Make sure (s)he does not rush through questions. (There is no prize for finishing first!) Tell your child to look carefully at the question. Then, tell your child to look at each answer choice before marking his/her answer.
    - If you notice your child continuing to rush through the questions, tell him/ her to point to each part of the question. Then, point to each answer choice.
- If (s)he does not know the answer, then use the process of elimination. Cross out any answer choices which are clearly incorrect, then choose from those remaining.
- This tip/suggestion is entirely at your discretion. You may wish to offer some sort of special motivation to encourage your child to do his/her best. An extra incentive of, for example, an art set, a building block set, or a special outing can go a long way in motivating young learners!
- The night before testing, it is imperative that children have enough sleep, without any interruptions. (Think about the difference in your brain function with a good night's sleep vs. without. The same goes for your child's brain function.)
- The morning before the test, ensure your child eats a healthy breakfast with protein and complex carbs. Do not let them eat sugar, chocolate, etc.
- If you can choose the time your child will take the test (for example, if (s)he will take the test individually, instead of at school with a group), opt for a morning testing session, when your child will be most alert.

QUESTION EXAMPLES - FOR PARENTS

- Here is an overview of the nine COGAT® question types..
- Below the questions are explanations.
- If you wish to go through this with your child, you may. Note, however, that the design of some sections of pages 6-11 are meant for parents/educators and may be confusing for kindergartners.

1. PICTURE ANALOGIES (VERBAL BATTERY)

- **Directions (read to child):** The pictures in the top boxes go together in some way. Look at the bottom boxes. One box is empty. Look at the row of pictures next to the boxes. These are the answer choices. Which one of these choices goes with the picture in the bottom box like the pictures in the top boxes go together?

- **Explanation:** Your child must figure out how the images in the top set of boxes are related and belong together. Then, (s)he must figure out which answer choice would go with the bottom left image so that the bottom set would have the same analogous relationship as the top set. (The small arrows demonstrate that the images go together.)

- One strategy is to try to define a "rule" to describe how the top set belongs together. Then, take this "rule" and use it with the bottom picture. Look at the answer choices, and figure out which answer would make the bottom set follow your "rule."

- **Using the above question as an example, say to your child:**
In this question, we see a bird and a nest. A bird's home is its nest. A rule would be, "the thing in the first box has as its home the thing in the second box." On the bottom we see a spider. Let's try the answer choices with our rule. A bird cage is not correct because a spider's home is not a bird care, nor is it another bird. A web is correct because it's a spider's home.

- Another similar strategy is to try to come up with a sentence to describe how the top set belongs together. Then, use this sentence with the bottom picture. Look at the answer choices, and figure out which answer would make the sentence work with this bottom set. With both strategies, if more than one answer choice works, then you need a more specific rule/sentence.

- The table below outlines the logic used in verbal analogies. This table is simply to familiarize you with analogy logic. You may read the questions and answers to your child, if you wish. However, do not worry if your child misses answers. The COGAT® Level 5/6 uses **pictures** (not words) in analogies. Again, this is meant simply as an introduction to analogy logic.

Question (say below & each 'Choice' to child)	Choice 1	Choice 2	Choice 3	Analogy Logic
1. Bird -is to- Nest as Spider -is to- ?	Cage	Bird	Web ✓	Animal: Animal's Home
2. Acorns -are to- Squirrel as Seeds -are to- ?	Bird ✓	Fish	Snake	Animal: Animal's Food
3. Calf -is to- Cow as Cub -is to- ?	Tiger ✓	Goose	Bull	Animal Baby: Animal Adult
4. Lion -is to- Fur as Snake -is to- ?	Hair	Fangs	Scales ✓	Animal: Animal's Covering
5. Happy -is to- Sad as Wet -is to- ?	Clean	Water	Dry ✓	"X": "X"'s Opposite
6. Tiger -is to- Cheetah as Butterfly -is to- ?	Bat	Moth ✓	Jaguar	Similar: Similar

Question (say below & each 'Choice' to child)	Choice 1	Choice 2	Choice 3	Analogy Logic
7. Flower -is to- Bouquet as Kernel -is to- ?	Plant	Corn Cob ✓	Crop	Part: Whole
8. Ship -is to- Port as Car -is to- ?	Garage ✓	Marina	Wheel	Object: Location
9. Pencil -is to- Paper as Paint -is to- ?	Wall ✓	Red	Light	Object: Object Used With
10. Lumber -is to- Fence as Paper -is to- ?	Branch	Tree	Book ✓	Object: Product That Object Is Put Together To Make
11. Artist -is to- Paint Brush as Carpenter -is to- ?	Builder	Cabinet	Hammer ✓	Worker Who Uses Object: Object
12. Cheese -is to- Refrigerator as Ice -is to- ?	Toaster	Freezer ✓	Cube	Object: Item Used to Store/Hold Object
13. Box -is to- Cube as Globe -is to- ?	Sphere ✓	Oval	Pentagon	Object: Similar Shape
14. Straw -is to- Juice as Spoon -is to- ?	Cereal ✓	Steak	Sandwich	Utensil: Object Utensil Is Used With
15. Egg -is to- Chicken as Milk -is to- ?	Cheese	Rooster	Cow ✓	Food/Drink: Source of Food/Drink
16. Spaceship -is to- Astronaut as Tractor -is to- ?	Garden	Scientist	Farmer ✓	Vehicle: User

2. PICTURE CLASSIFICATION (VERBAL BATTERY)

• **Directions (read to child):** The top row shows three pictures that are alike in some way. Look at the bottom row. There are three pictures. Which picture in the bottom row goes best with the pictures in the top row?

• **Explanation (for parents):** Together with your child, try to figure out a "rule" describing how the top pictures are alike and belong together. Then, apply the "rule" to each answer choice to determine which one follows it. If your child finds that more than one choice follows the rule, then a more specific rule is needed.

• **Using the above question as an example, say to your child:** In the top row, we see a cake, a cookie, and a piece of candy. What do these have in common? Each of these is a type of sweet. This is how they are alike. The only answer choice that is also a sweet is the ice cream.

You can help your child improve classification using items you see in everyday life or in books. The table on the next page lists common themes for Picture Classification (which also appear in Picture Analogies and Sentence Completion questions). Under the logic is an example question. It is meant simply as an introduction to these common themes.

- If you wish, you may read the questions and answers to your child. Do not worry if your child misses answers. The COGAT® Level 5/6 uses **pictures** (not words). Again, this table is meant only to familiarize you with question logic.

Read the first list of 3 words to your child. Then, next to it, read the 3 choices to your child. Which one of the choices goes best with the first list?

-Step 1: Read the three words on the left to your child. Tell him/her that these words belong together in some way.

-Step 2: Read the three words on the right to your child. Ask him/her which one of these goes best with the first three words. The answer has a check (✓). Following is a brief explanation of the question's logic in *italics*.

Question (read to child)	Answer Choices (read to child)	Classification Logic / Explanation
1. Cave / Hive / Web	Spider / Nest ✓ / Bat	*Animal Homes*
2. Butterfly / Ant / Bee	Worm / Bird / Dragonfly ✓	*Animal Types (Insects)*
3. Forest / Jungle / Desert	Tree / Valley / Rainforest ✓	*Habitats*
4. Lemon / Grape / Apple	Strawberry ✓ / Sweet / Lettuce	*Kinds of Food (Fruit)*
5. Scientist / Nurse / Detective	Superhero / Pilot ✓ / Fairy	*Jobs*
6. Sock / Skate / Boot	Slipper ✓ / Mitten / Toe	*Clothes/Shoes (Worn on Feet)*
7. Jet / Hot Air Balloon / Helicopter	Ship / Bird / Airplane ✓	*Transportation (Air Travel)*
8. Ruler / Scale / Measuring Tape	Thermometer ✓ / Number / TV	*Object Use (Used to Measure)*
9. Pillow / Blanket / Mattress	Towel / Chair / Sheet ✓	*Object Location (Found on Beds)*
10. Fire / Sun / Stove	Cookie / Toaster ✓ / Beach	*Object Characteristics (Give Heat)*
11. Planet / Ball / Globe	Country / Bubble ✓ / Racetrack	*Object Shape (Spherical)*

3. SENTENCE COMPLETION (VERBAL BATTERY)

- **Directions (read to child):** Listen to the question, then choose the best answer.

Which one of these shows something you would wear?

○   ○   ○

- **Explanation (for parents):** Unlike Picture Analogies and Picture Classification, Sentence Completion questions have different directions for each question. (The answer is C.) This question is very simple. The questions in the practice tests will be more challenging.

- It is imperative that your child listens carefully to these questions. COGAT® administrators will not repeat the questions.

- If listening is challenging for your child - tell him/her to repeat the directions back to you.

- Remind your child to listen to the entire question. (Some children will stop listening if they think they already know the answer.)

- Tell him/her to pay special attention to "negative" words like "not" or "no." (The two practice tests include questions like this.)

4. FIGURE ANALOGIES (NON-VERBAL BATTERY)

• **Directions (read to child):** The pictures in the top boxes go together in some way. Look at the bottom boxes. One box is empty. Look at the row of pictures next to the boxes. These are the answer choices. Which one of these choices goes with the picture in the bottom box like the pictures in the top box go together?

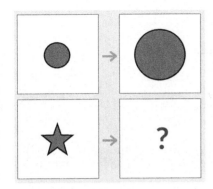 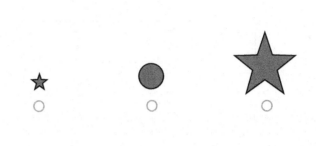

• **Explanation:** In the directions, the word "picture" means a "figure" consisting of one or more shapes/lines/etc. As with Picture Analogies, try to define a "rule" to describe how the top set belongs together. With Figure Analogies, however, make your "rule" describe a "change" that occurs from the top left box to the top right box. Next, take this "rule" describing the change, and apply it to the bottom picture. Then, look at the answer choices to determine which one would make the bottom set also follow your "rule."

• **Using the above question as an example, say to your child:** In the top left box, we see 1 circle. In the top right box, we also see a circle, but it has gotten bigger. Let's come up with a rule to describe how the picture has changed from left to right. From left to right, the shape gets bigger. On the bottom is a star. Let's look at the answer choices and see if any fit our rule. The first choice does not - the shape is smaller. The second choice does not - it is a different shape. The last choice does - it is the same shape as the bottom box, but it is bigger.

• Below are examples of basic "changes" seen in Figure Analogies. See if your child can explain the changes below. At the end is a brief explanation.

 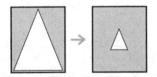

2.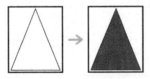

3.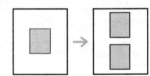

4.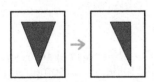

5.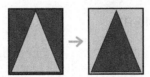

6.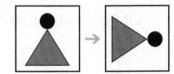

7.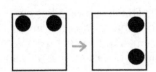

8.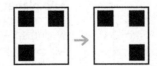

9.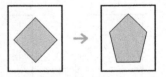

10.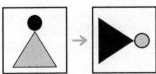

1. Size (gets smaller)
2. Color (white to gray)
3. Quantity (plus 1)
4. Whole to Half
5. Color Reversal
6. Rotation (clockwise, 90°)

7. Rotation (clockwise, 90°)
8. Rotation -or- Mirror Image / "Flip"
9. Number of Shape Sides (shape with +1 side)
10. Two Changes: Rotation (clockwise, 90°)
   & Color Reversal. This is a challenging one.
   Don't worry about wrong answers.

5. FIGURE CLASSIFICATION (NON-VERBAL BATTERY)

• **Directions (read to child):** The top row shows three pictures that are alike in some way. Look at the bottom row. There are three pictures. Which picture in the bottom row goes best with the pictures in the top row?

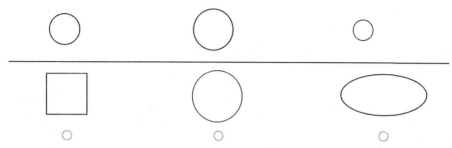

• **Explanation (for parents):** Together with your child, try to figure out a "rule" describing how the top pictures are alike and belong together. Then, apply the "rule" to each answer choice to determine which one follows it. If your child finds that more than one choice follows the rule, then a more specific rule is needed.

• **Using the above question as an example, say to your child:** What shapes do we see on the top row? We see 3 circles of different sizes. What is a rule that describes how they are alike? They are all circles. In the bottom row, which choice follows this rule? Choice 1 is a square. Choice 2 shows a circle. Choice 3 is an oval.

This list outlines some basic logic used in Figure Classification questions.

How shapes are divided (Here, shapes are divided in quarters, with 1 part filled in.)	
How many sides the shapes have (Here, it is 4.)	
Do shapes have rounded outlines or straight outlines? (Here, they are rounded.)	
Direction shapes are facing (Here, they face right.)	
Color / Design inside shape (Here, there are dots.)	
Shape quantity in each shape group (Here, 2 shapes in each group.)	
How are the circles divided? (They are divided in half.)	

6. PAPER FOLDING (NON-VERBAL BATTERY)

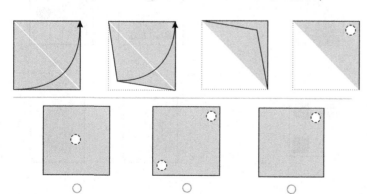

• **Directions (read to child):** The top row of pictures shows a sheet of paper. The paper was folded, then something was cut out. Which picture in the bottom row shows how the paper would look after its unfolded?

• **Explanation (read to child):** The first choice has an incorrect number of holes. It only has 1. Plus, it is in the wrong spot. The second choice has the correct number of holes and in the correct position. The last choice only shows the hole on top.

• **Tip:** It is common for children to initially struggle with Paper Folding - it is not an activity most children have much experience with. First, have a look at the Paper Folding questions in this book. Then, demonstrate using hands-on examples. Get sheets of real paper, and let your child experiment with:

- different fold directions (horizontal, vertical, diagonal)   - different placement of holes

7. NUMBER SERIES (QUANTITATIVE BATTERY)

- **Directions (read to child):** Which rod should go in the place of the missing rod to finish the pattern?

- **Explanation (read to child):** Before the missing rod, the other rods have made a pattern that we need to figure out. Then, we will complete the pattern with the correct answer choice. From left to right, we see that with each rod the number of beads goes down by 1. The rods go: 5–4–3-2- ? This means that the missing rod needs 1 bead (Choice C).

Below is a list of common Number Series patterns.

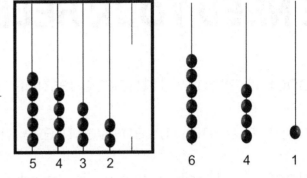

Basic Patterns	Number of Beads
• +1	1, 2, 3, 4, 5
• -1	5, 4, 3, 2, 1
• A/B/A/B	1, 2, 1, 2
• A/B/C/D/C/B/A	1, 2, 3, 4, 3, 2, 1

8. NUMBER PUZZLES (QUANTITATIVE BATTERY)

- **Directions (read to child):** Which train car should you choose so that the top train is carrying the same number of items as the bottom train?

- **Explanation:** The top train carries four items (four hearts). The bottom train carries two items. Next to the train car with two hearts is a train car with a question mark. Which train car from the answer choices should be put here so that the bottom train would have the same number of items (hearts) as the top train? It would be the choice with 2 hearts (choice A).

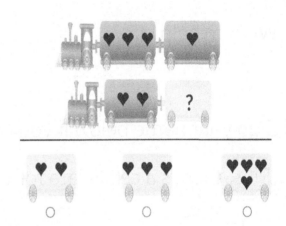

9. NUMBER ANALOGIES (QUANTITATIVE BATTERY)

- **Directions (read to child):** The pictures in the top boxes go together in some way. Look at the bottom boxes. One box is empty. Look at the row of answer choices next to the boxes. Which one of these choices goes with the picture in the bottom box like the pictures in the top box go together?

- **Explanation (read to child):** In the left box there are 2 objects (stars). In the right box there is 1 object. From left to right, we see that 1 object has been taken away. So, the rule here is "1 is taken away." In the bottom left box there are 3 objects. If our rule is "1 is taken away," if you have 3 and you take away 1, you get 2. The second answer choice is correct.

- **Tip:** Some analogies involve addition and subtraction, while others require children to do more complex calculations: dividing in half or doubling. If your child first tries to add or subtract, but no answer choice matches the "rule," then try to double or triple (if the number increases from left to right) or try to halve (if the number decreases from left to right).

Show your child this example. In the top left box are 2 stars. In the top right box is 1 star. Let's try the rule "take away 1." In the bottom left box are 4 stars. If our rule is "take away 1," then the answer should be 3 stars. However, there isn't an answer choice with 3 stars. Let's look again at the top boxes. What is half of 2? Half of 2 is 1. Let's try the rule "half." What is half of 4? Half of 4 is 2. Choice A has 2 stars.

WE NEED YOUR HELP!

(Parents read to kids.)

LUCAS

This book is filled with tricky questions. We need someone super-smart to help us answer these mind-bending questions. We think that super-smart person is <u>**you**</u>.

Will you help us?

Sign your name below if you can help, and let's get started!

(Plus, there's a certificate for you at the end of the book.)

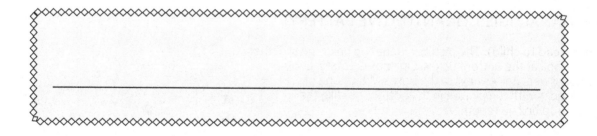

AMY   **JACK**   **AVA**   **ROHAN**   **LEE**

LET'S HELP AMY! WHAT GOES IN THE EMPTY BOX?

PICTURE ANALOGIES

Directions (read to child): The pictures in the top boxes go together in some way. Look at the bottom boxes. One box is empty. Look at the row of pictures next to the boxes. These are the answer choices. Which one of these choices goes with the picture in the bottom box like the pictures in the top boxes go together?

Explanation (for parents): A more detailed explanation and another example question are on p. 6. If you have not already, look over p. 6 (later). Following is an excerpt.

Your child must figure out how the images in the top set of boxes are related and belong together. Then, (s)he must figure out which answer choice would go with the bottom left image so that the bottom set would have the same analogous relationship as the top set. (The small arrows demonstrate that the images go together.)

Example (read this to child): Look at the boxes on top. In the first box, we see mittens. In the second box we see gloves. (Together, try to come up with a "rule" describing how they are alike and go together.) Mittens are worn on hands. Gloves are worn on hands. The things in the first box and the second box are similar. Also, they are both worn on the same place. Let's look in the bottom box. We see a sock. Now, let's look at the answer choices. Which one goes with the picture of a sock in the same way that the pictures in the top row go together? The sock with dots (the second choice).

Parent note: A common mistake for kids would be to pick an answer that only "has to do with" the top row. (Here, the glove "has to do with" the top row.) Another common mistake is picking an answer that simply "has to do with" the bottom left box, but does not actually follow the rule of the relationship. Here, a foot "has to do with" a sock, but it does not follow the rule, and it does not have the same relationship.

EXAMPLE:

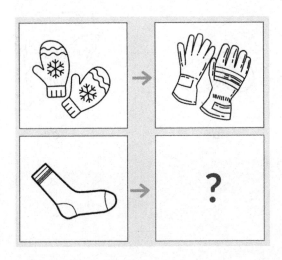

Ⓐ

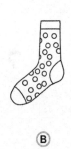

Ⓑ

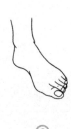

Ⓒ

1.

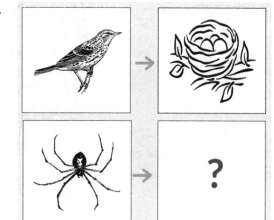

(A)

(B)

(C)

2

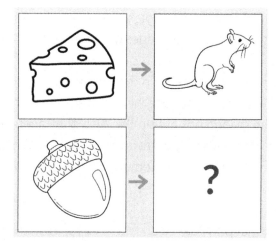

(A)

(B)

(C)

3.

(A)

(B)

(C)

4.

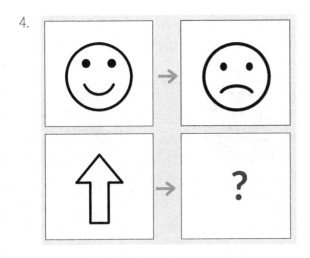

    A

   B

    C

5.

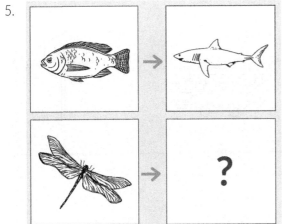

   A   B   C

6.

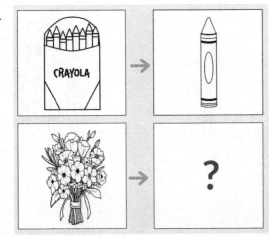

   A

   B

   C

7.

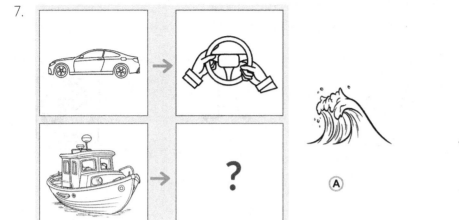

(A)

(B)

(C)

8.

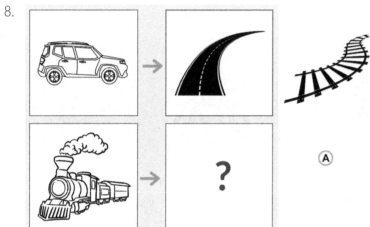

(A)

(B)

(C)

9.

(A)

(B)

(C)

10.

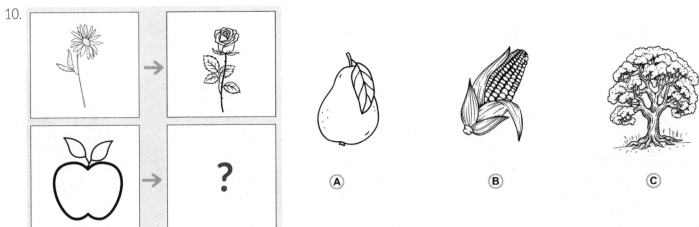

11.

12.

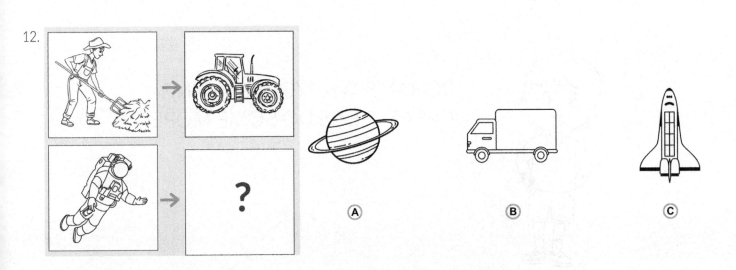

13.

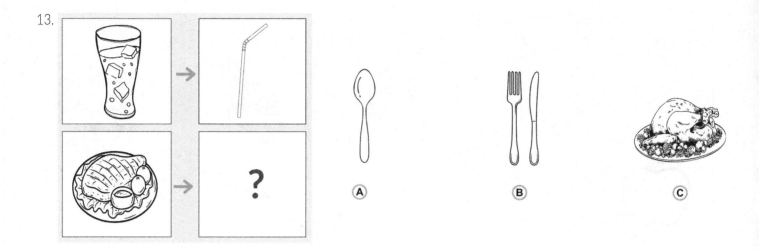

(A) (B) (C)

14.

(A) (B) (C)

ROHAN SAYS, "YOU'RE DOING GREAT - LET'S DO SOME MORE!"

WILL YOU HELP JACK AND LEE?
THESE QUESTIONS ARE HARD!
WHAT GOES IN THE BOX?

FIGURE ANALOGIES

Directions (read to child): The pictures in the top boxes go together in some way. Look at the bottom boxes. One box is empty. Look at the row of pictures next to the boxes. These are the answer choices. Which one of these choices goes with the picture in the bottom box like the pictures in the top boxes go together?

Explanation (for parents): A more detailed explanation and a Figure Analogies example question is on p. 9. If you have not already, look over p. 9 (later). Try to define a "rule" to describe how the top set belongs together. With Figure Analogies, this "rule" could describe a "change" that occurs from the top left box to the top right box. Next, take this "rule" describing the change, and apply it to the bottom picture.

Example (read this to child): In the first box, we see a white triangle. In the second box we see a triangle, but now it is gray. Our rule is that the shape from the first box changes and becomes gray.

Let's look in the bottom box. We see a white circle. Which answer choice follows our rule? The choice that shows a gray circle is the correct answer.

EXAMPLE:

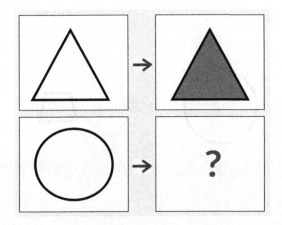

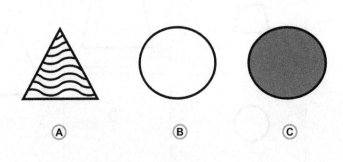

Ⓐ   Ⓑ   Ⓒ

1.

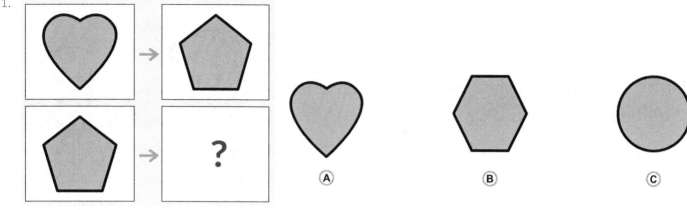

2.

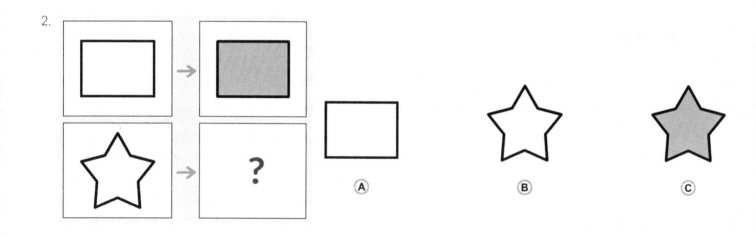

3.

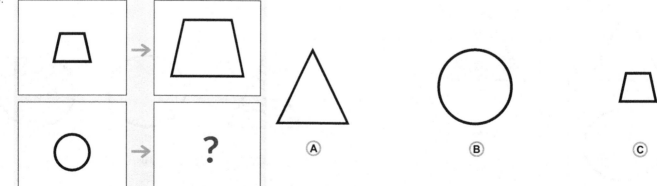

4

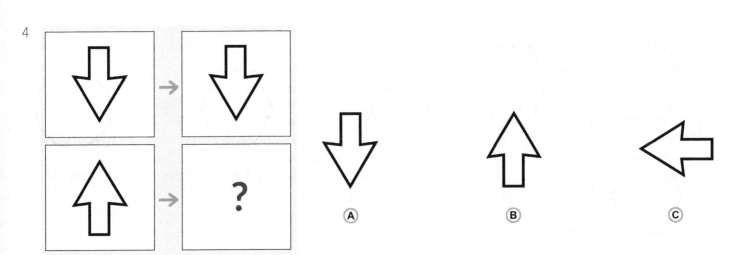

5.

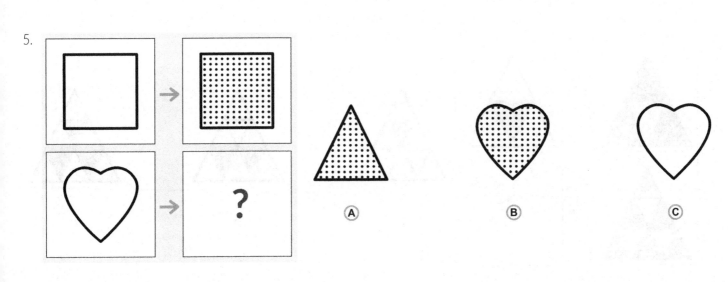

6.

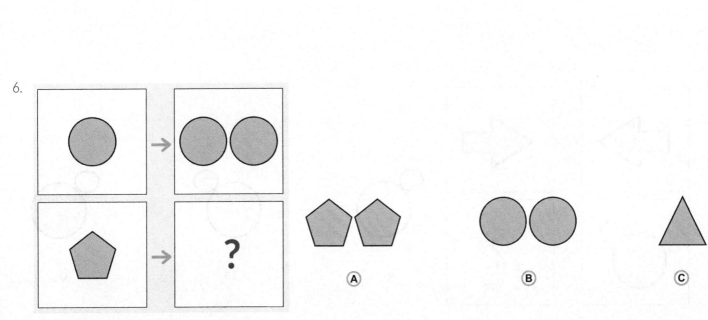

7.

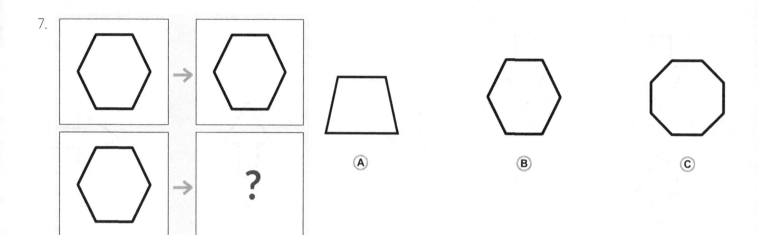

8.

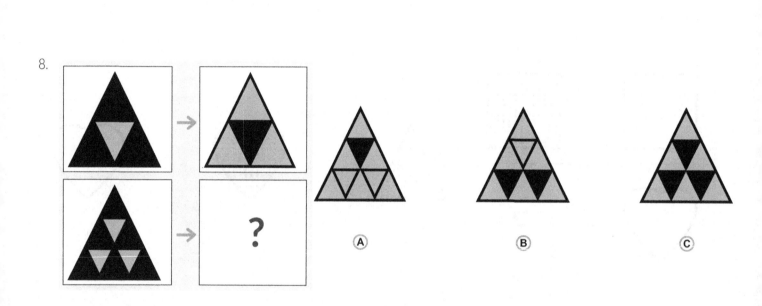

9.

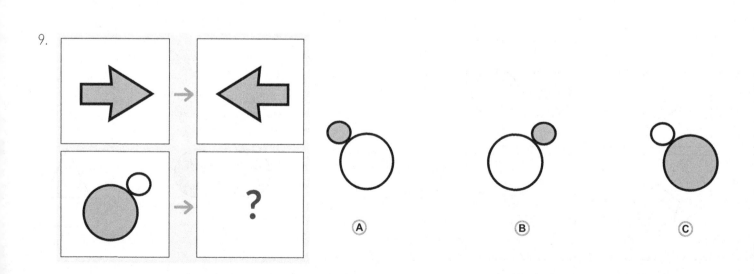

10.

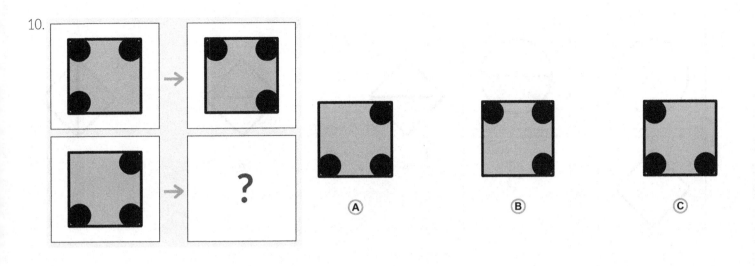

11.

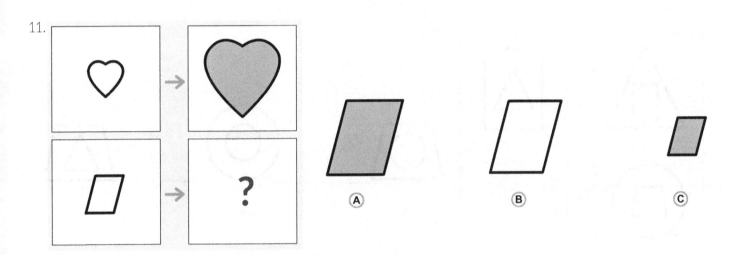

12.

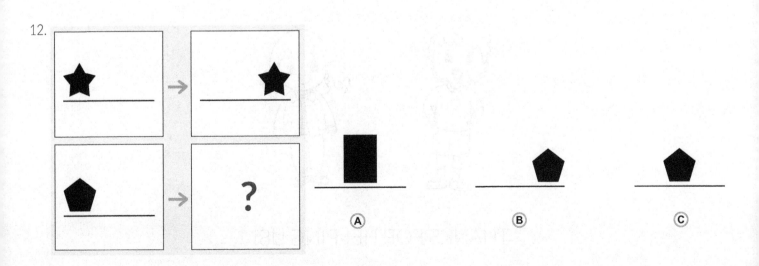

23

13.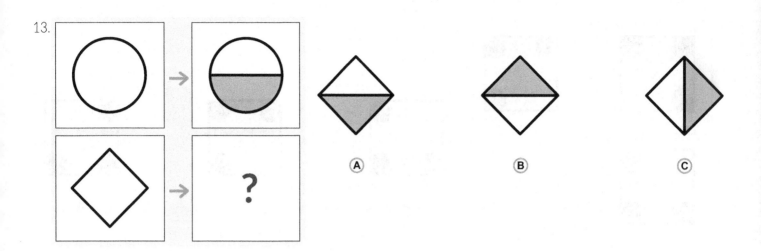

14.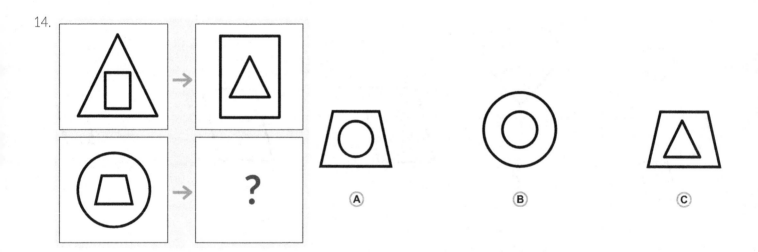

THANKS FOR HELPING US!

TIME TO HELP AVA!

PICTURE CLASSIFICATION

Directions (read to child):
The top row shows three pictures that are alike in some way. Look at the bottom row. There are three pictures. Which picture in the bottom row goes best with the pictures in the top row?

Explanation (for parents):
A more detailed explanation and another Picture Classification example question is on p.7. If you have not already, look over p. 7 (later). Following is an excerpt. Together with your child, try to figure out a "rule" describing how the top pictures are alike and belong together. Then, apply the "rule" to each answer choice to determine which one follows it. If your child finds that more than one choice follows the rule, then a more specific rule is needed.

Example (read to child):
Let's look at the pictures on the top row. We see lettuce, a carrot, and broccoli. Let's come up with a "rule" to describe how these are each alike or how they belong together.

These are all vegetables. Now, let's look at the bottom row. Let's find the answer choice on the bottom that follows this same rule of things that are vegetables. We see an apple, a strawberry, and corn.

Which one of these goes best with the pictures in the top row? Which one of them is a vegetable? The corn.

EXAMPLE:

Ⓐ
Ⓑ
Ⓒ

1.

Ⓐ Ⓑ Ⓒ

2.

Ⓐ Ⓑ Ⓒ

3.

Ⓐ Ⓑ Ⓒ

4.

Ⓐ Ⓑ Ⓒ

5.

Ⓐ Ⓑ Ⓒ

6.

Ⓐ Ⓑ Ⓒ

7.

(A) (B) (C)

8.

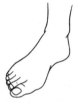

  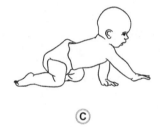

(A) (B) (C)

9.

(A) (B) (C)

10.

(A)	(B)	(C)

11.

(A)	(B)	(C)

12.

(A)	(B)	(C)

13.

Ⓐ

Ⓑ

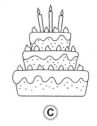

Ⓒ

14.

Ⓐ

Ⓑ

Ⓒ

FANTASTIC WORK!

LET'S DO SOME MORE.

WILL YOU HELP ROHAN ANSWER THESE?

FIGURE CLASSIFICATION

Directions (read to child): The top row shows three pictures that are alike in some way. Look at the bottom row. There are three pictures. Which picture in the bottom row goes best with the pictures in the top row?

Explanation (for parents): A more detailed explanation of Figure Classification questions is on p. 10. If you have not already, look over p. 10 (later). Following is an excerpt.

Together with your child, try to figure out a "rule" describing how the top pictures are alike and belong together. Then, apply the "rule" to each answer choice to determine which one follows it.

If your child finds that more than one choice follows the rule, then a more specific rule is needed. The "rule" for number 1 would be "is a triangle". Choice B is the answer.

EXAMPLE:

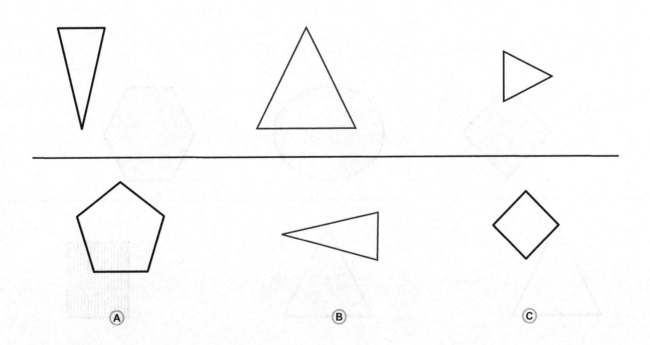

1

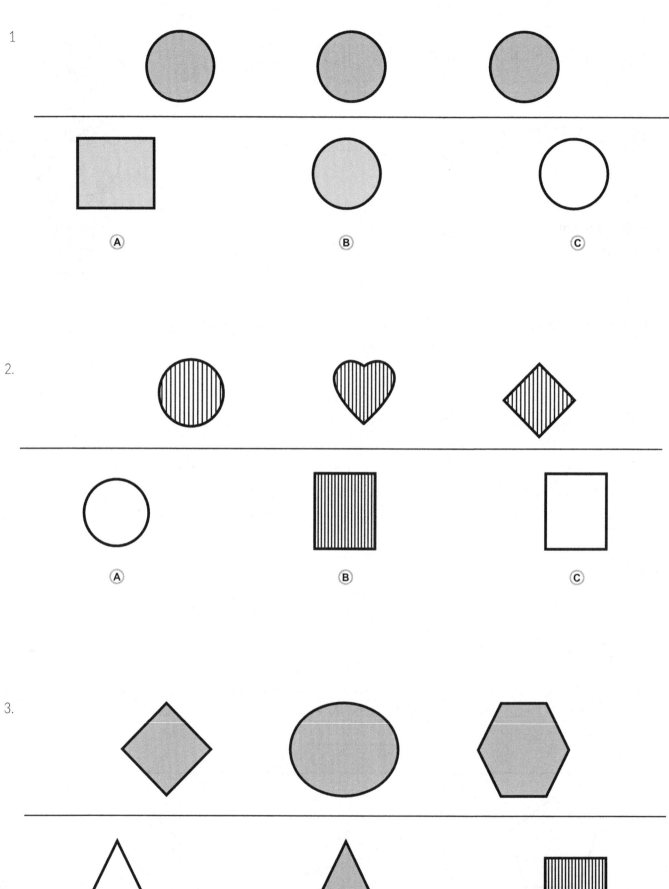

A   B   C

2.

A   B   C

3.

A   B   C

4.

Ⓐ   Ⓑ   Ⓒ

5.

Ⓐ   Ⓑ   Ⓒ

6.

Ⓐ   Ⓑ   Ⓒ

7.

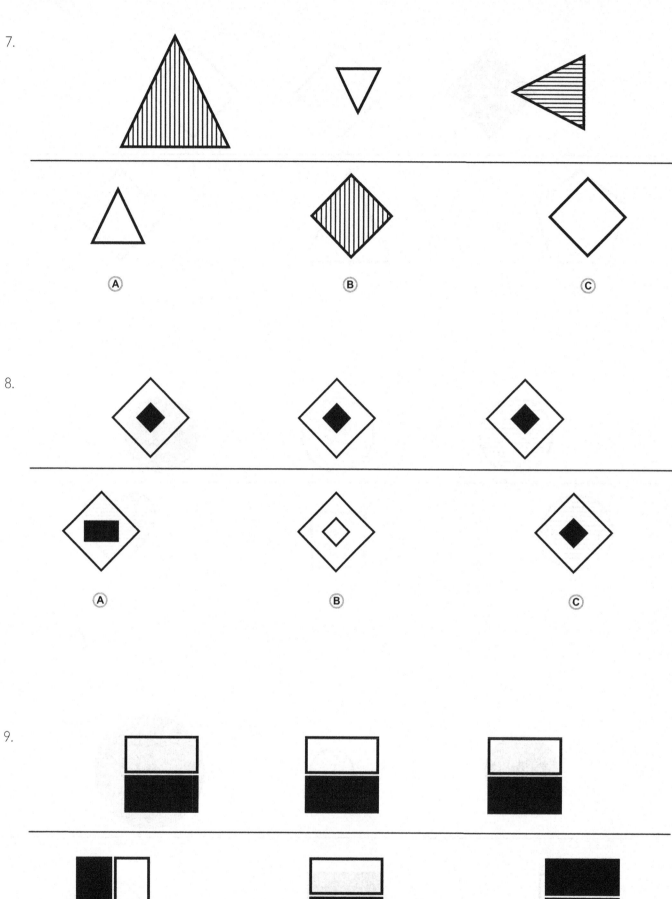

A   B   C

8.

A   B   C

9.

A   B   C

34

10.

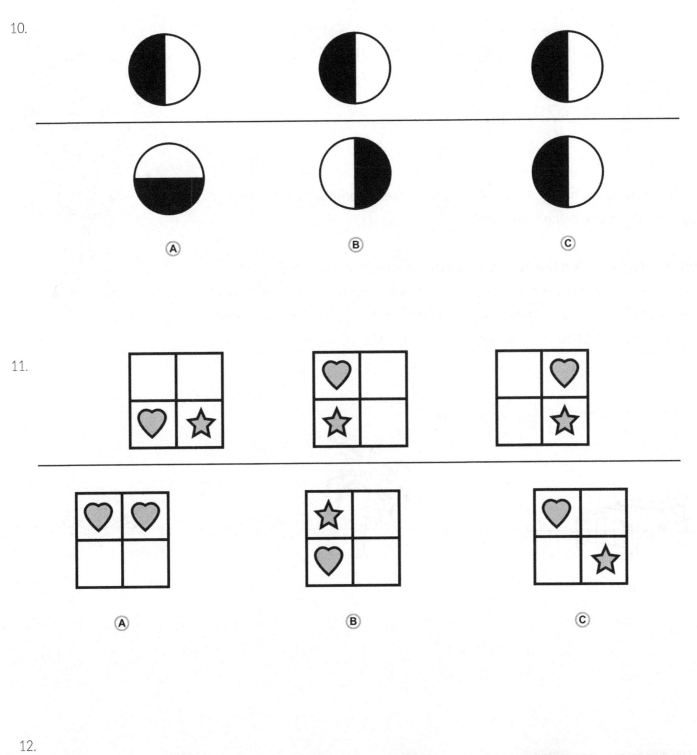

(A)　　　　　　(B)　　　　　　(C)

11.

(A)　　　　　　(B)　　　　　　(C)

12.

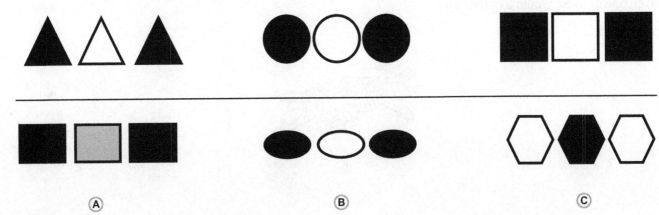

(A)　　　　　　(B)　　　　　　(C)

LUCAS SAYS, "WILL YOU HELP ME NEXT?"

SENTENCE COMPLETION

Directions (read to child): Listen to the question, then choose the best answer. I can only read the question one time.

Additional information (for parents): Read the questions below to your child. As explained earlier in the Introduction on p. 8, test administrators will read these questions only one time. Therefore, it is imperative that your child practice careful listening skills, so that you will not need to repeat the questions.

1. Which one of these would you see in a kitchen?

Ⓐ

Ⓑ

Ⓒ

2. Which one of these would a farmer use?

Ⓐ

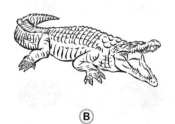
Ⓑ

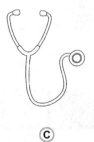
Ⓒ

3. Which one of these can fly in the air?

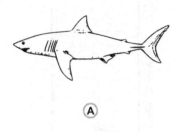

Ⓐ

Ⓑ

Ⓒ

4. If it were cold outside, which one of these would be best to wear?

Ⓐ

Ⓑ

Ⓒ

5. If you were at the beach, which one of these animals would you see?

Ⓐ

Ⓑ

Ⓒ

6. Which one would you use if you needed to heat something up?

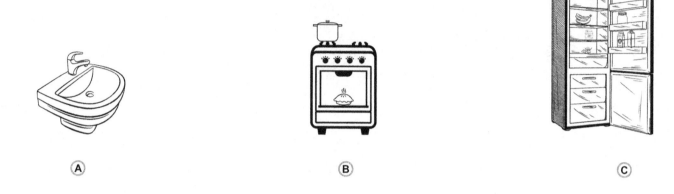

7. Which one of these comes from a tree?

8. If you needed to measure how long something was, which one would be best to use?

9. Which one of these would a baby calf belong to?

(A)

(B)

(C)

10. If you were in the desert, which animal would you not see?

(A)

(B)

(C)

11. If you were in a classroom, which of these would you not see?

(A)

(B)

(C)

12. Which one of these shows a pair?

Ⓐ

Ⓑ

Ⓒ

13. If you saw an animal swimming, which one would it be?

Ⓐ

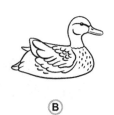

Ⓑ

Ⓒ

14. If you needed to check the time, which one of these would you not look at?

Ⓐ

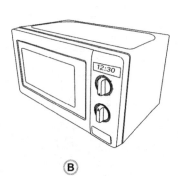

Ⓑ

Ⓒ

AMY SAYS, "I'M GLAD YOU'RE HERE. THESE ARE TRICKY!"

PAPER FOLDING

Directions: Look at the top row of pictures. These show a sheet of paper and how it was folded. Look at these pictures that are on the bottom row. Which picture shows how the paper would look after the paper is unfolded?

Parent note: Below are 2 "warm-up" examples. The actual paper folding exercises may be challenging at first. If so, practicing using a real sheet of paper will help your child visualize how these questions work.

EXAMPLES:

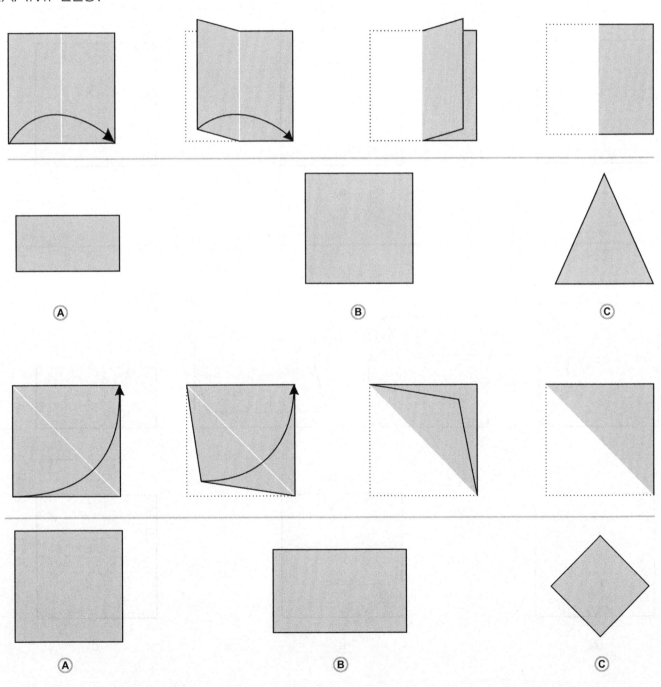

Directions (read to child): The top row of pictures shows a sheet of paper. The paper was folded, then something was cut out. Which picture in the bottom row shows how the paper would look after its unfolded?

1.

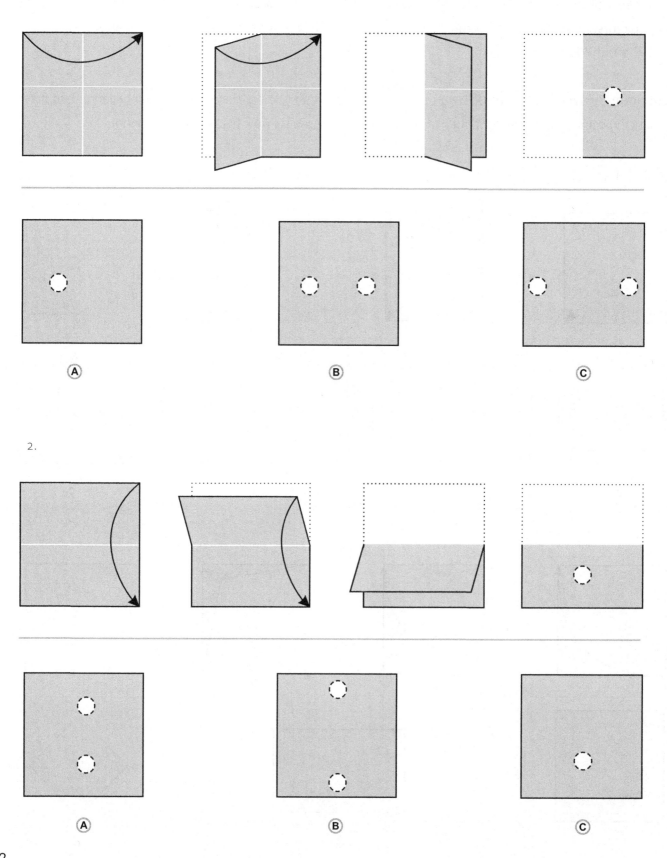

3.

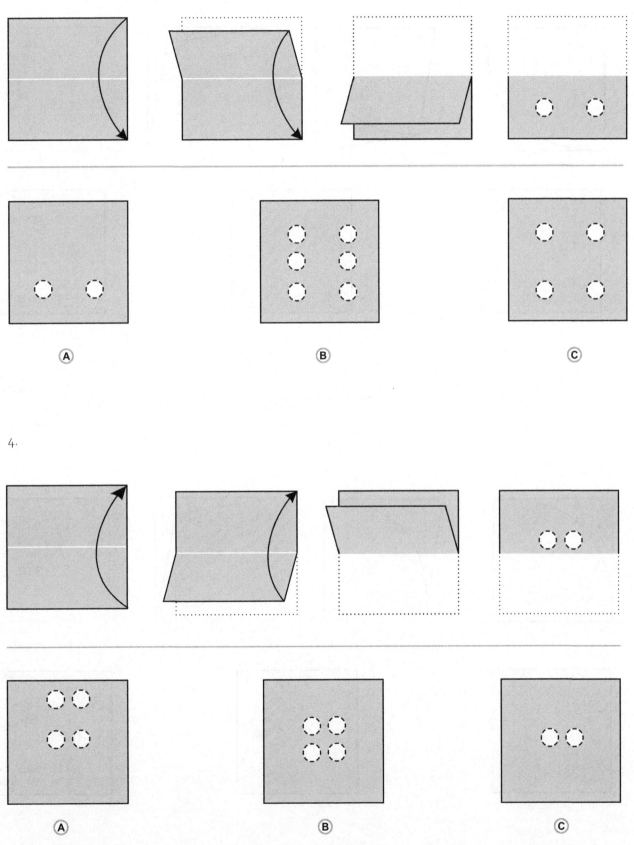

4.

5.

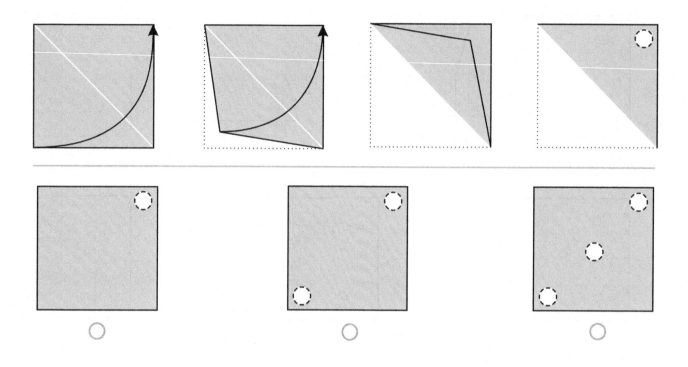

6.

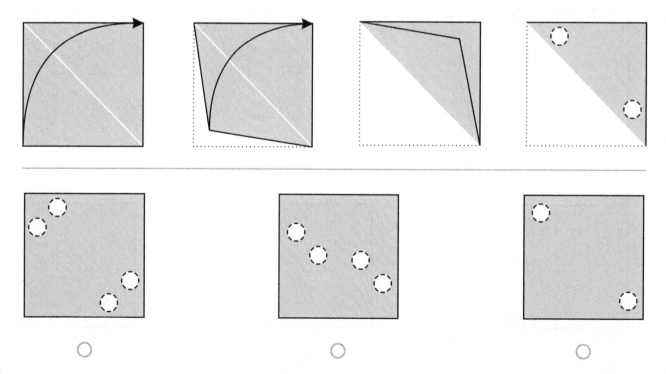

7.

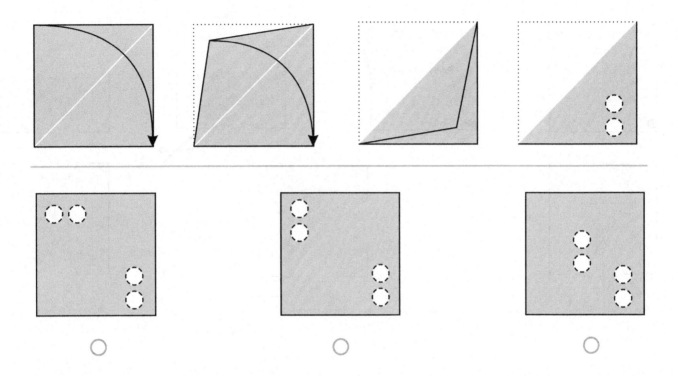

Directions: Look at the top row of pictures. These show a sheet of paper and how it was folded. The picture with the scissors shows where a part of the folded sheet of paper was cut out. On the bottom row, which picture shows how the sheet of paper would look after the paper is unfolded?

8.

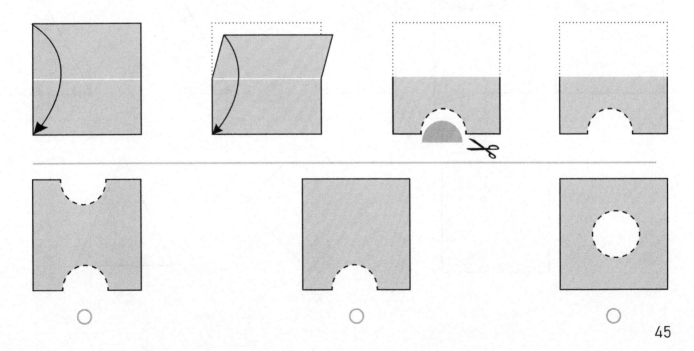

9.

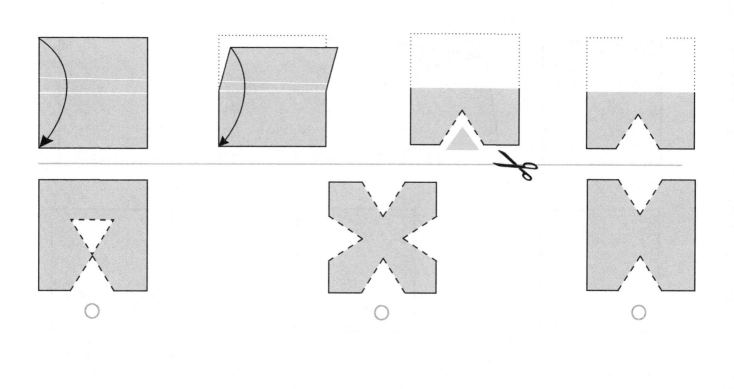

○   ○   ○

10.

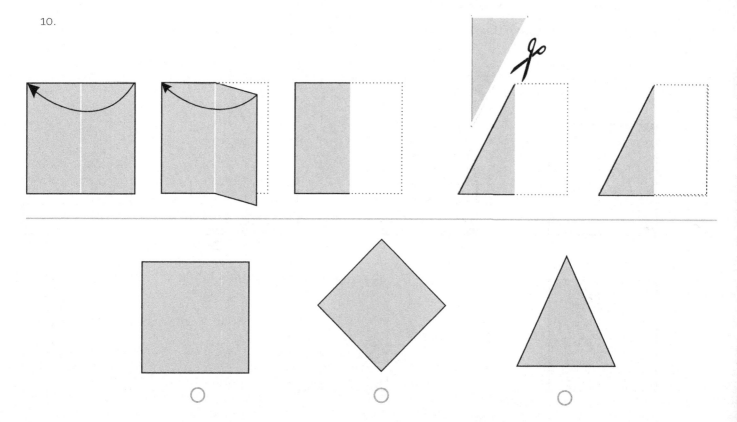

○   ○   ○

46

JACK SAYS, "AM I HAPPY TO SEE YOU! LET'S TRY TO FIGURE THESE OUT."

NUMBER PUZZLES

Info for Parents: "Number Puzzles" questions consist of two trains - a top train and a bottom train. The top train must carry the same number of items as the bottom train. Children must use math skills to decide which answer choice goes in place of the train car with the question mark, so that the bottom train has the same number of items as the top train. Your child should carefully count the number of items the trains carry to avoid careless errors. Below are detailed directions for question #1.

Directions for Question #1 (read to child): Look at the top train. It has 3 squares. Look at the bottom train. The bottom train has 1 square in the left train car. The right train car has a question mark. We must figure out which train car in the answer choices would go in place of the train car with the question mark so that the top train and the bottom train have the same number of hearts. Remember that the top train has 3 hearts. So, the bottom train car on the right must have 2 hearts. One plus two equals 3. Which answer choice has 2 squares? Choice B is the answer.

Directions for the rest (read to child): Which train car should you choose so that the top train has the same number of items as the bottom train?

EXAMPLE:

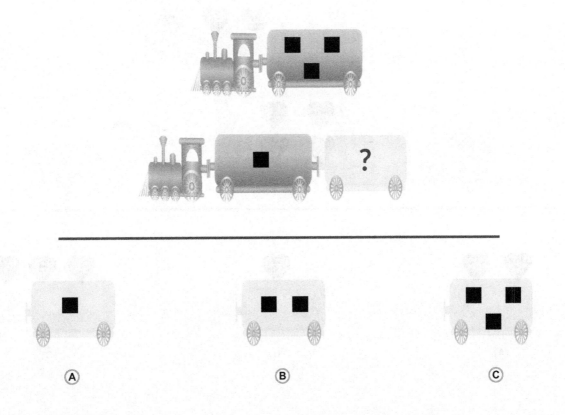

Ⓐ   Ⓑ   Ⓒ

1.

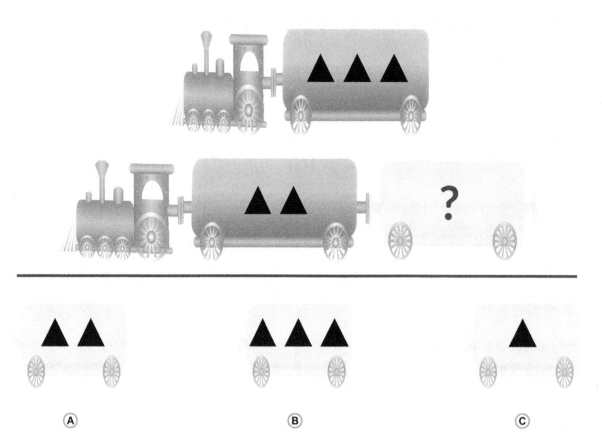

(A)   (B)   (C)

2.

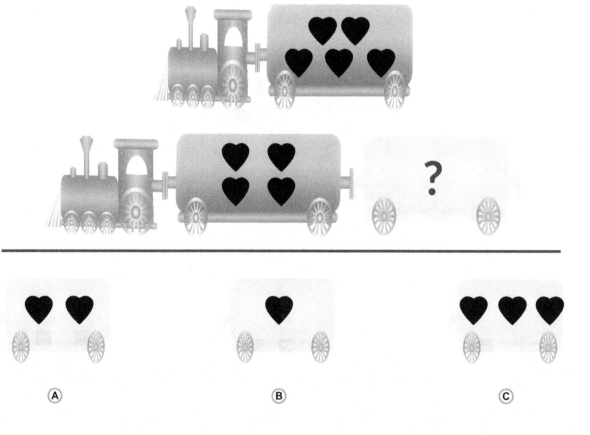

(A)   (B)   (C)

3.

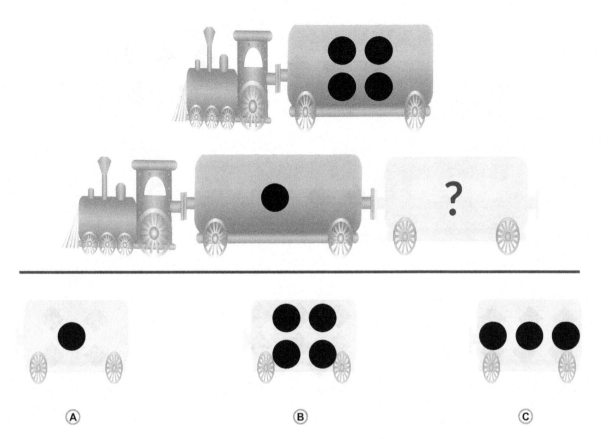

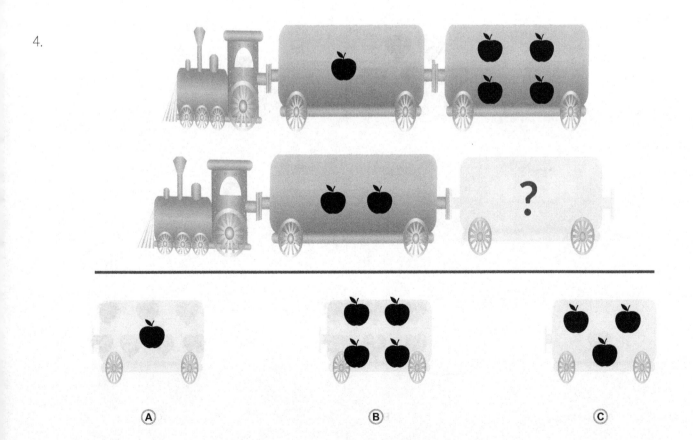

(A) (B) (C)

4.

(A) (B) (C)

5.

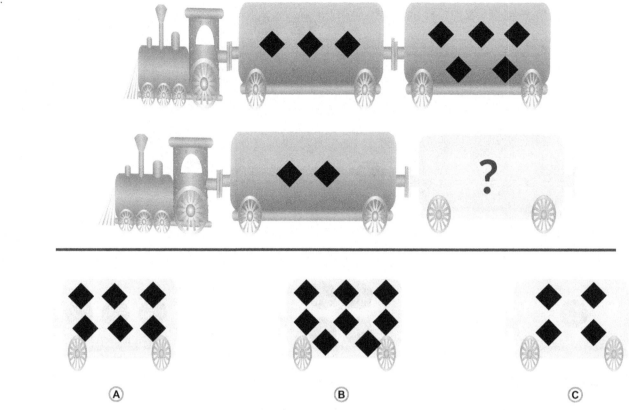

Ⓐ Ⓑ Ⓒ

6.

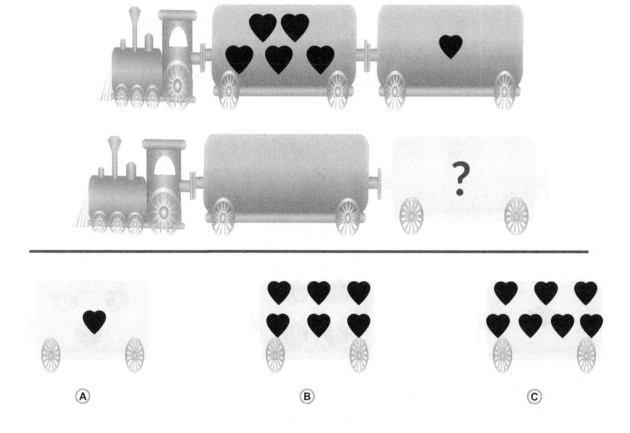

Ⓐ Ⓑ Ⓒ

7.

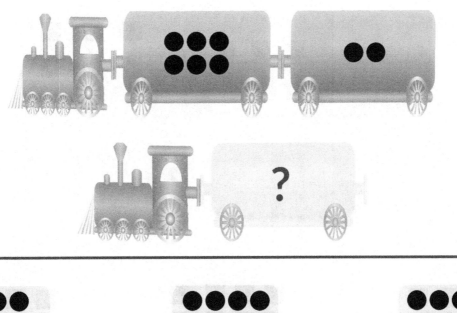

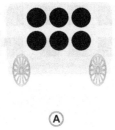  

(A)   (B)   (C)

8.

(A)   (B)   (C)

9.

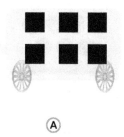

Ⓐ   Ⓑ   Ⓒ

10.

Ⓐ   Ⓑ   Ⓒ

LEE SAYS, "I'M GLAD YOU SHOWED UP. LET'S SEE IF WE CAN COME UP WITH AN ANSWER TO THESE!"

NUMBER SERIES

Directions (read to child): Which rod should go in the place of the missing rod to finish the pattern?

Explanation (for parents): The final rod of the abacus is missing. Before this missing rod, the rods of the abacus have made a pattern. Your child must look closely to determine the pattern.

Note that some rods do not have any beads. Rods without any beads equal "0". The gray line appears above the 5th bead's place.

Example (read to child): Let's look at this picture below. It shows an abacus. The abacus has rods going bottom to top. On these rods are beads. These rods have made a pattern that we need to figure out.

First, we see a rod with 1 bead. Then, we see 2 beads, 1 bead, 2 beads, and 1 bead. Then, finally there is a missing rod. What is the pattern that these rods have made? The rods switch between having 1 bead, 2 beads, 1 bead, and 2 beads.

If this is the pattern, what should the next rod be (the rod that would go in place of the missing rod on the abacus)? The rod with 2 beads, choice C.

EXAMPLE:

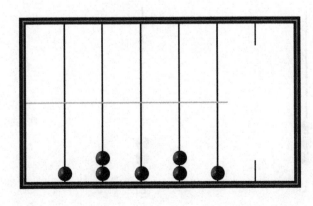

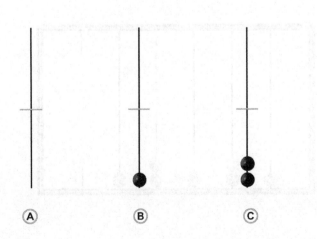

1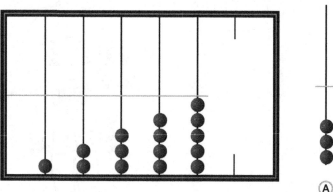

Ⓐ Ⓑ Ⓒ

2.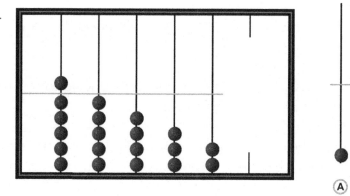

Ⓐ Ⓑ Ⓒ

3.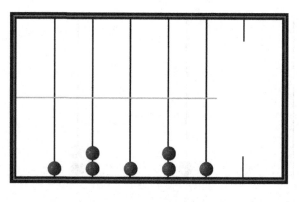

Ⓐ Ⓑ Ⓒ

4.

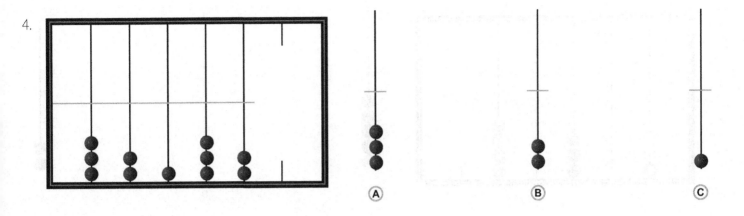

5.

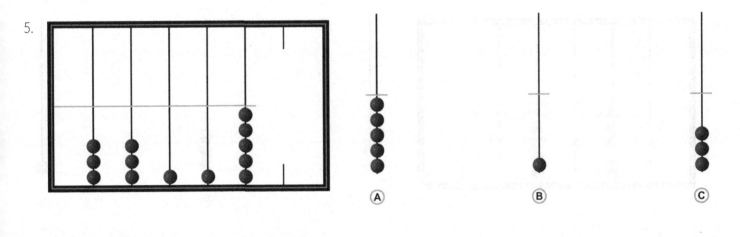

6.

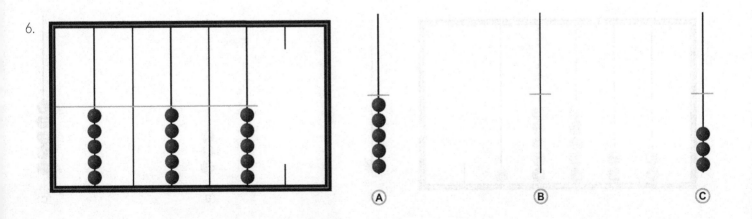

55

7.

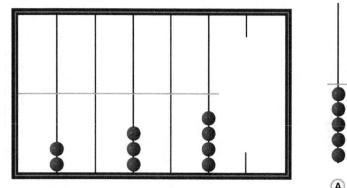  

Ⓐ   Ⓑ   Ⓒ

8.

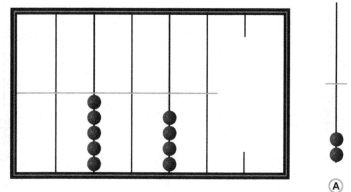 

Ⓐ   Ⓑ   Ⓒ

9.

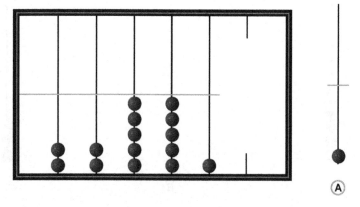  

Ⓐ   Ⓑ   Ⓒ

10.

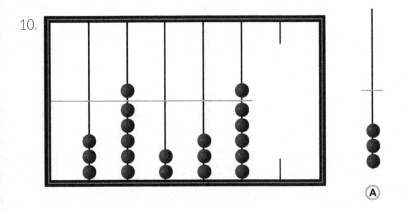 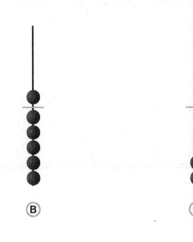

11.

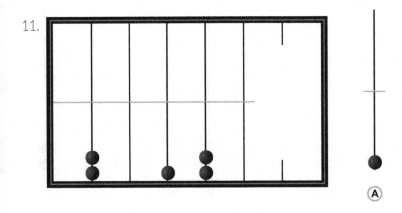 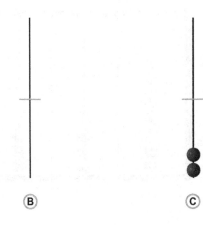

12.

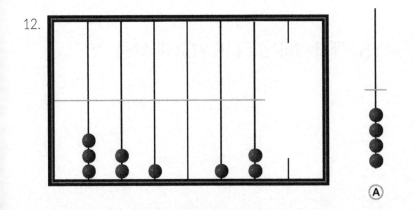 

13.

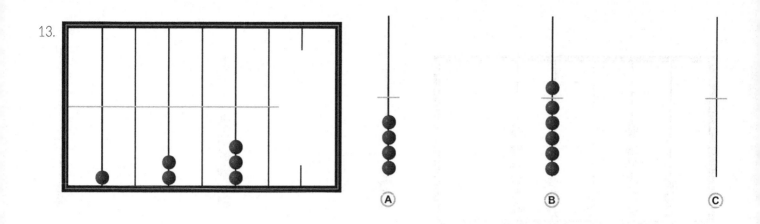

A   B   C

14.

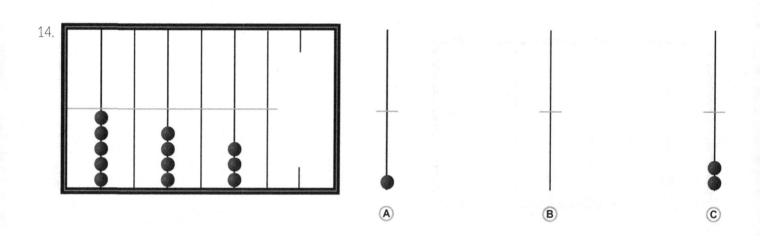

A   B   C

LEE SAYS, "THANKS FOR YOUR HELP!"

ROHAN SAYS, "GREAT! WE ARE ALMOST DONE
WITH THE FIRST PART. I KNOW WE CAN DO THIS!"

NUMBER ANALOGIES

Explanation (for parents): A more detailed explanation and example questions are on p. 11. Look over p.11 (later), if you have not already. Your child must figure out how the images in top set of boxes are related mathematically. Then, (s)he must figure out which answer choice would go with the bottom left image so that the bottom set would have the same relationship. For example, the mathematical relationship in the example question is "plus one." After counting the objects in the boxes, you may want your child to write the number by the box, so (s)he does not forget the quantity.

Directions for the example: The top boxes belong together in some way. Look at the top box on the left. There is one juice box. Look at the top box on the right. There are two juice boxes. What has changed from the picture on the left to the picture on the right? We need to come up with a "rule" to describe what has happened. The right box will have one more than the left box.

Next, let's look carefully at the bottom row. What do you see in the left box? There are 4 apples. Look at the right box. It is empty. Look carefully at the row of pictures next to the boxes. These are the answer choices.

Which one of these goes in the empty box? Remember, our rule is that the right box will have 1 more than the left box.

If the left box has 4 apples, and our rule is that the right box will have 1 more, then that means 5 apples is the answer. The last answer choice has 5 apples.

Directions for the rest: Which answer choice would go inside the empty box at the bottom?

EXAMPLE:

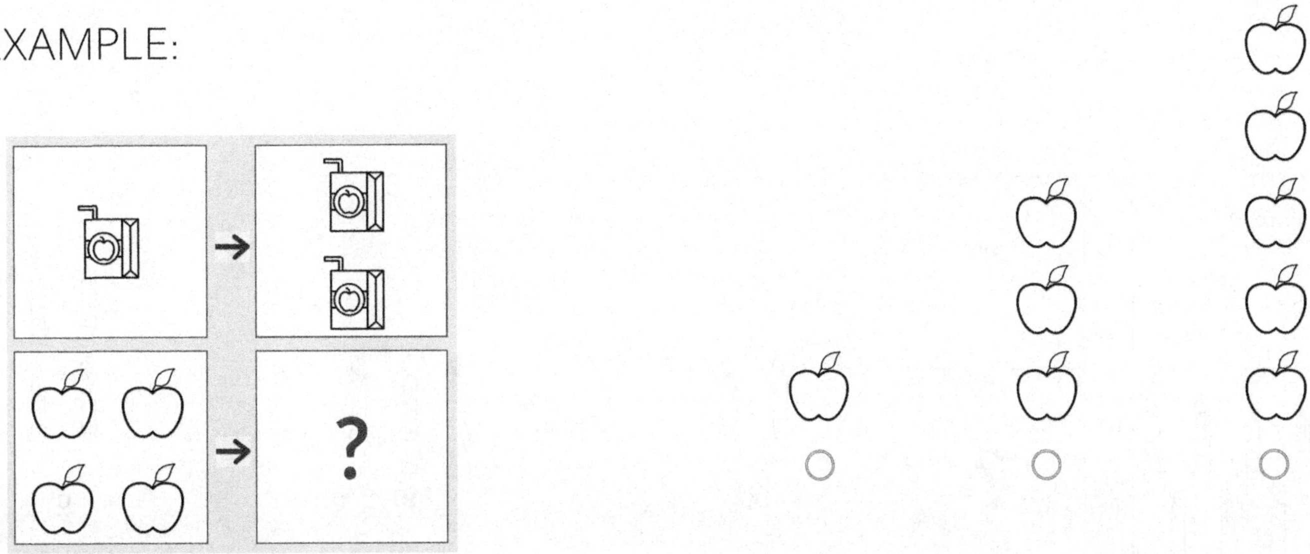

1.

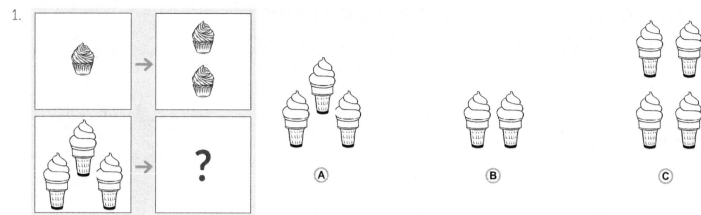

A   B   C

2.

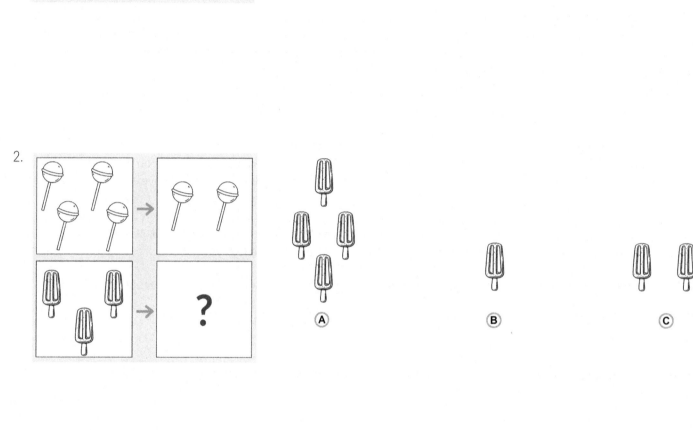

A   B   C

3.

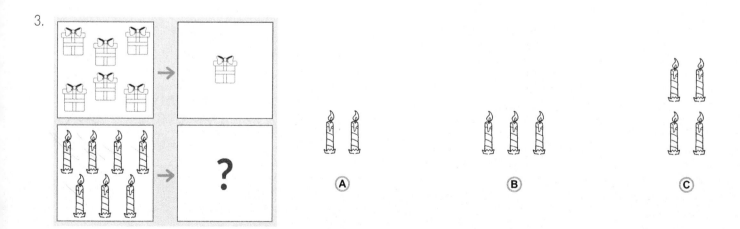

A   B   C

4.

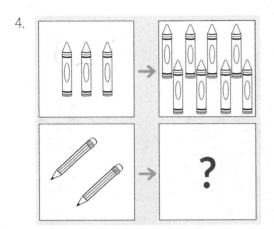 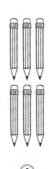 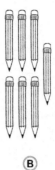 

Ⓐ　　　　　　　　Ⓑ　　　　　　　　Ⓒ

5.

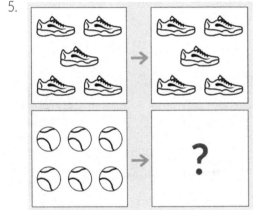

Ⓐ　　　　　　　　Ⓑ　　　　　　　　Ⓒ

6.

 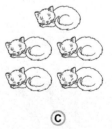

Ⓐ　　　　　　　　Ⓑ　　　　　　　　Ⓒ

7.

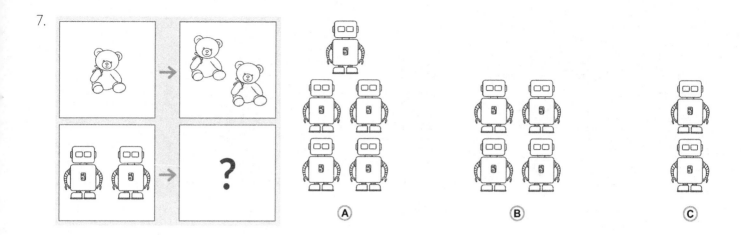

8.

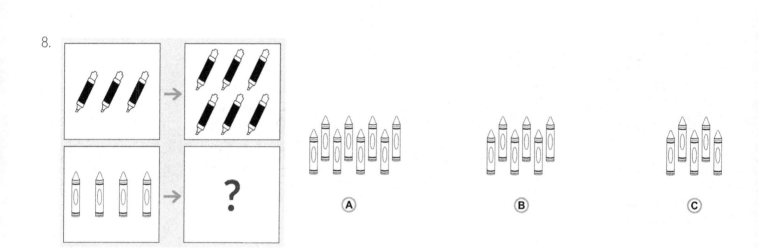

9.

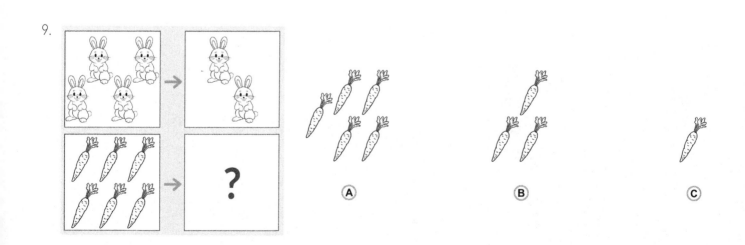

10.

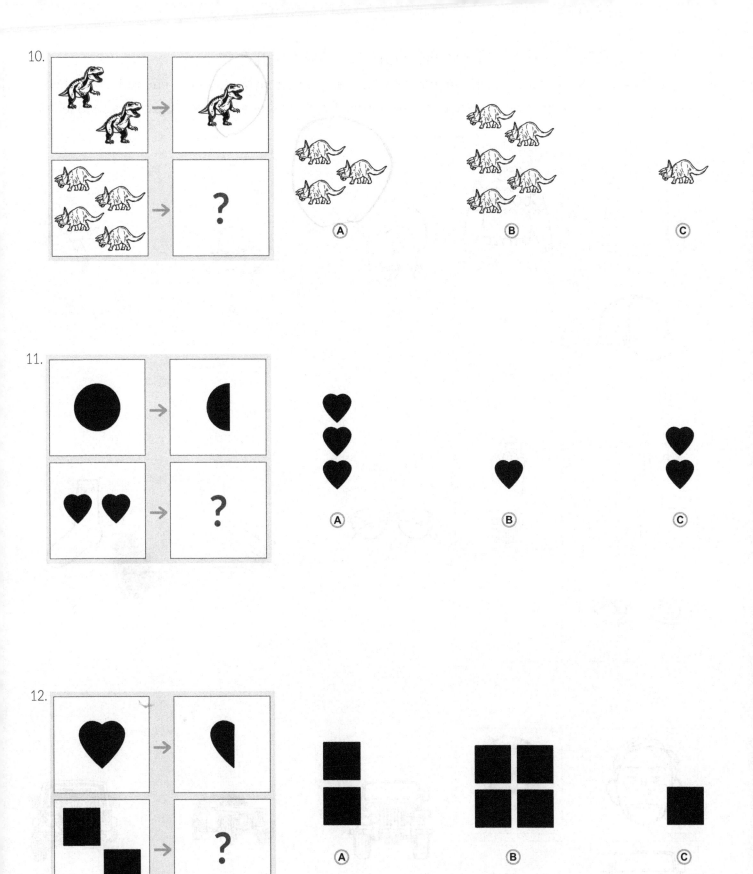

11.

12.

- End of Practice Test 1. -
- Practice Test 2 begins on the next page. -

START OF PRACTICE TEST 2 / PICTURE ANALOGIES

Directions: The pictures on top go together in some way. Look at the bottom boxes. One is empty. Look at the answer choices. Which one goes with the picture in the bottom box in the same way the top pictures go together?

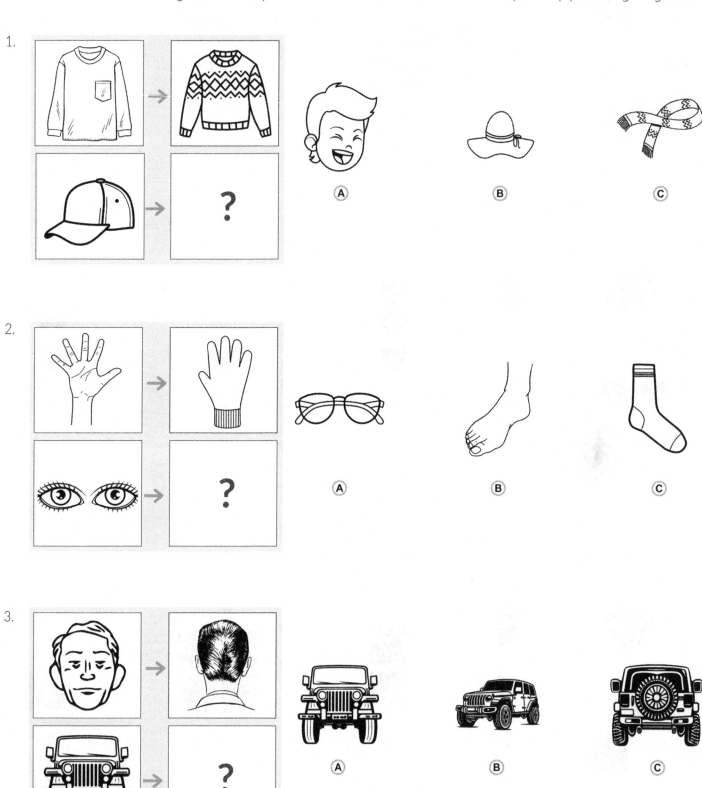

4.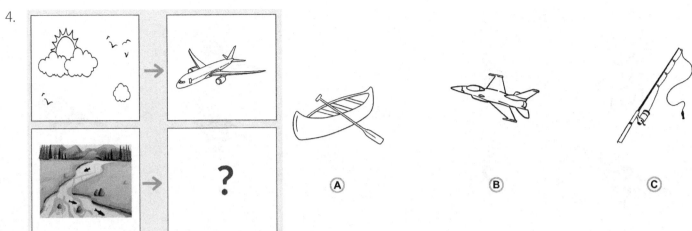

A   B   C

5.

6.

7.

Ⓐ   Ⓑ   Ⓒ

8.

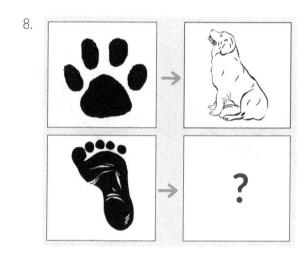

?

Ⓐ   Ⓑ   Ⓒ

9.

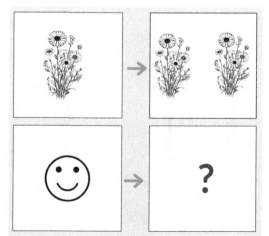

?

Ⓐ   Ⓑ   Ⓒ

10.

A   B   C

11.

A   B   C

12.

A   B   C

13.

14.

PICTURE CLASSIFICATION

Directions: The top row shows three pictures that are alike in some way. Look at the bottom row. There are three pictures. Which bottom picture goes best with the top pictures?

1.

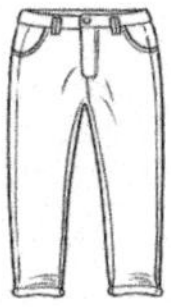

A   B   C

2.

A   B   C

3.

A   B   C

69

4.

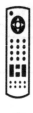 

Ⓐ Ⓑ Ⓒ

5.

Ⓐ Ⓑ Ⓒ

6.

 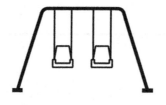

  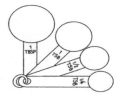

Ⓐ Ⓑ Ⓒ

7.

Ⓐ Ⓑ Ⓒ

8.

Ⓐ Ⓑ Ⓒ

9.

Ⓐ Ⓑ Ⓒ

71

10.

(A) (B) (C)

11.

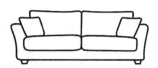 

(A) (B) (C)

12.

(A) (B) (C)

13.

Ⓐ Ⓑ Ⓒ

14.

Ⓐ Ⓑ Ⓒ

SENTENCE COMPLETION

Directions: Listen to the question, then choose the best answer.

1. Which one of these would float in water?

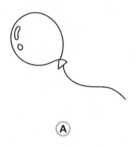
(A)

(B)

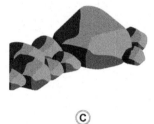
(C)

2. Which one of these would sink in water?

(A)

(B)

(C)

3. If you saw an animal climbing a tree, which animal would it be?

(A)

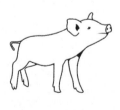
(B)

(C)

4. Which one of these would you not see while driving on a road?

(A)

(B)

(C)

5. Anna's favorite animal has paws. Which one of these is Anna's favorite animal?

(A)

(B)

(C)

6. If you were going to the store on a cold day, which one of these should you have?

(A)

(B)

(C)

7. Which one of these shows something that has been peeled?

Ⓐ

Ⓑ

Ⓒ

8. Which one of these is upside down?

Ⓐ

Ⓑ

Ⓒ

9. Which picture shows something that is not living?

Ⓐ

Ⓑ

Ⓒ

10. A grown-up needs something to cut down a tree. Which one would be the best to use?

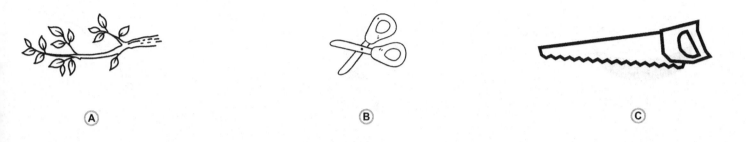

A   B   C

11. Which one of these helps keep you safe on a boat?

A   B   C

12. Which one would be the best to go from one city to another city?

A   B   C

13. Which one of these would break easily?

(A)

(B)

(C)

14. Which of these would you see in a tropical rainforest?

(A)

(B)

(C)

FIGURE ANALOGIES

Directions: The pictures on top go together in some way. Look at the bottom boxes. One is empty. Look at the row of answer choices. Which one goes with the picture in the bottom box like the pictures on top go together?

1

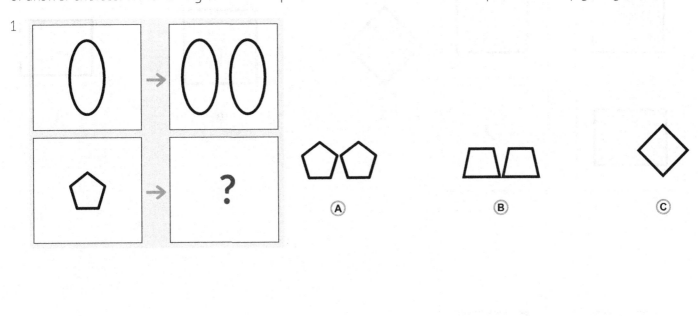

2

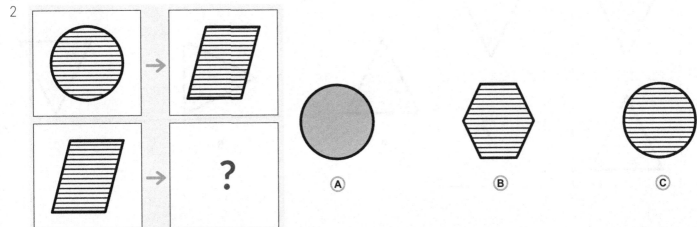

3.

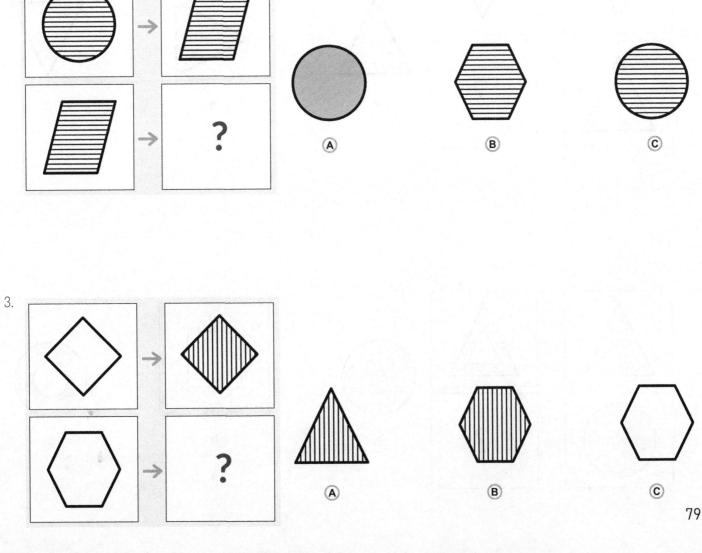

4.

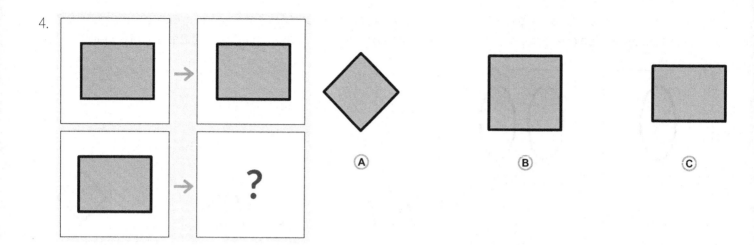

5.

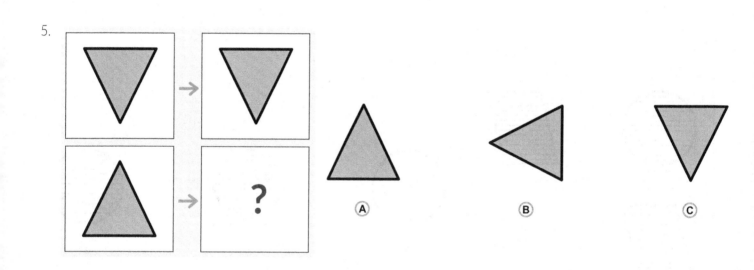

6.

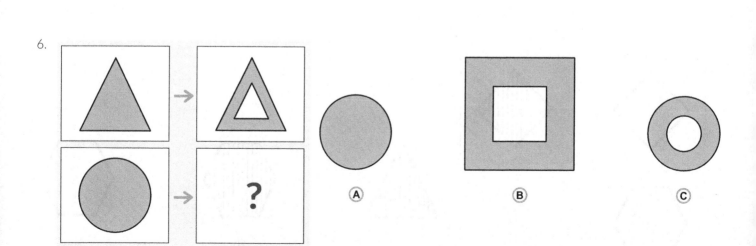

7

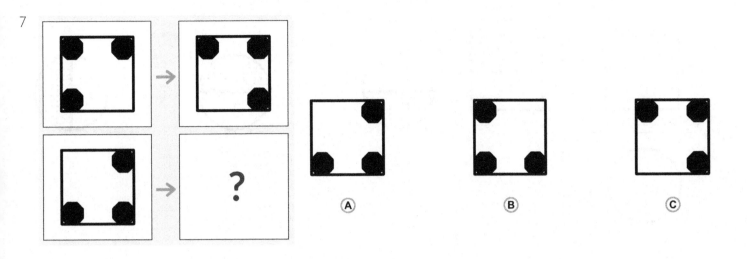

A   B   C

8.

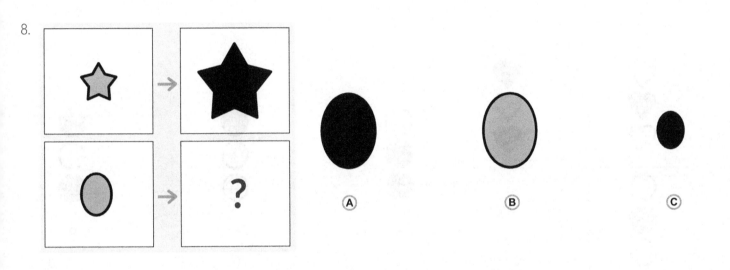

A   B   C

9.

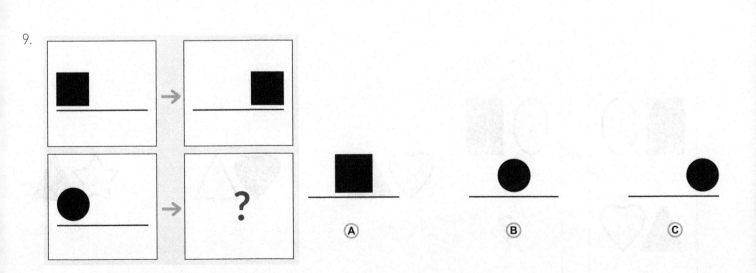

A   B   C

10.

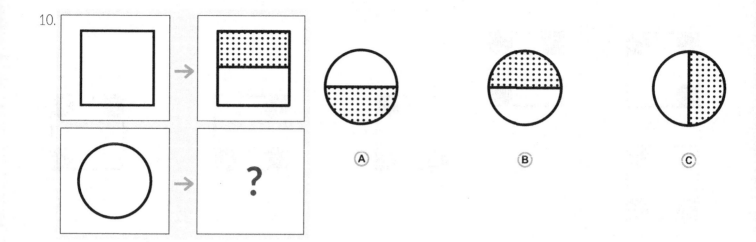

11.

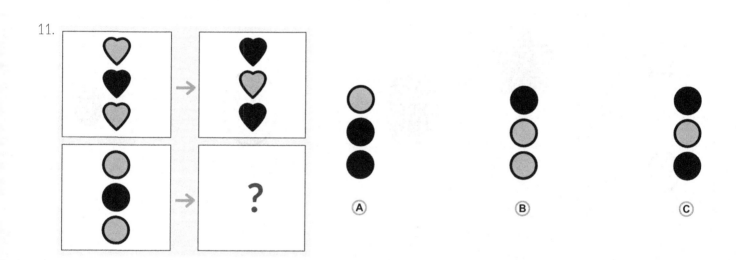

12.

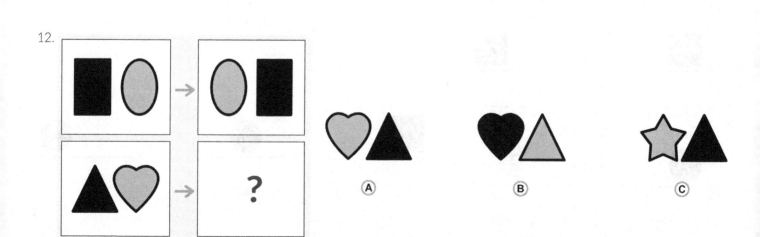

13.

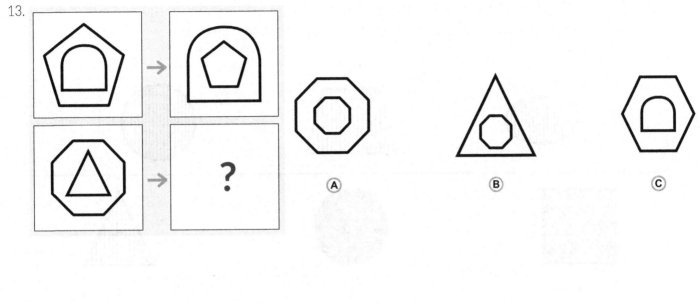

14.

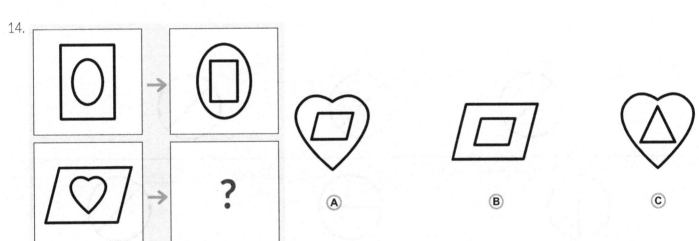

FIGURE CLASSIFICATION

Directions: The top row shows three pictures that are alike in some way. Look at the bottom row. There are three pictures. Which picture in the bottom row goes best with the pictures in the top row?

1.

A ⃝ B ⃝ C ⃝

2.

A ⃝ B ⃝ C ⃝

3.

A ⃝ B ⃝ C ⃝

4.

A   B   C

5.

A   B   C

6.

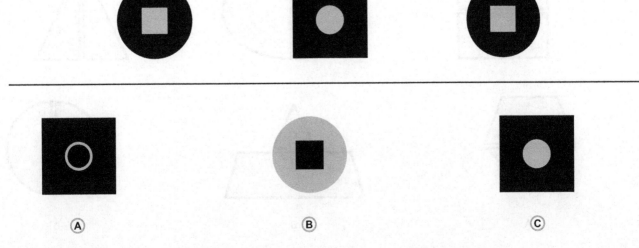

A   B   C

85

7.

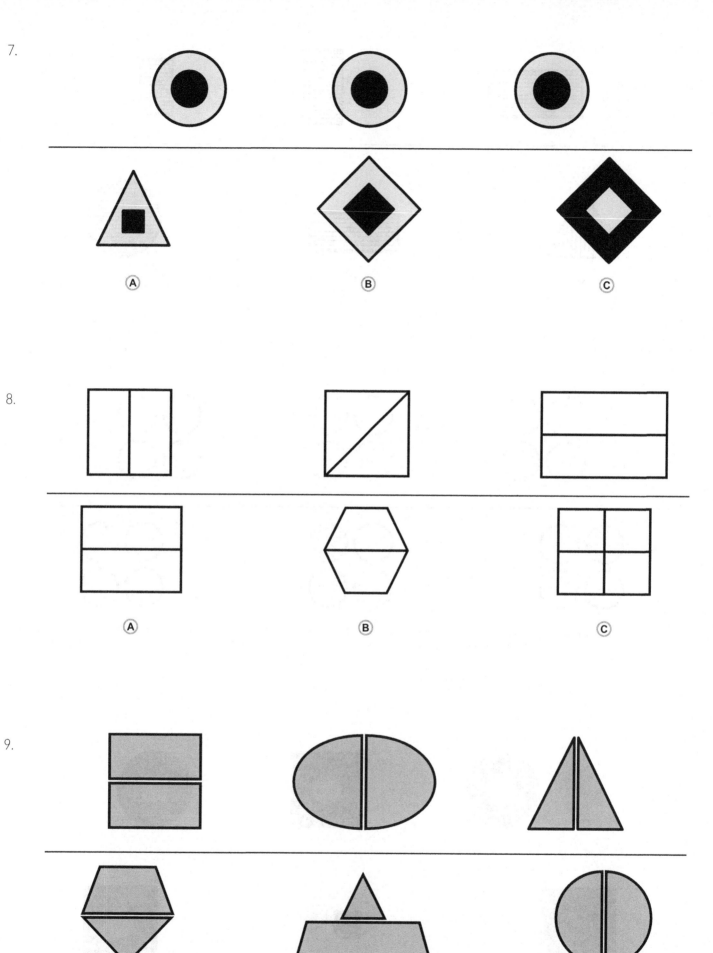

A

B

C

8.

A

B

C

9.

A

B

C

86

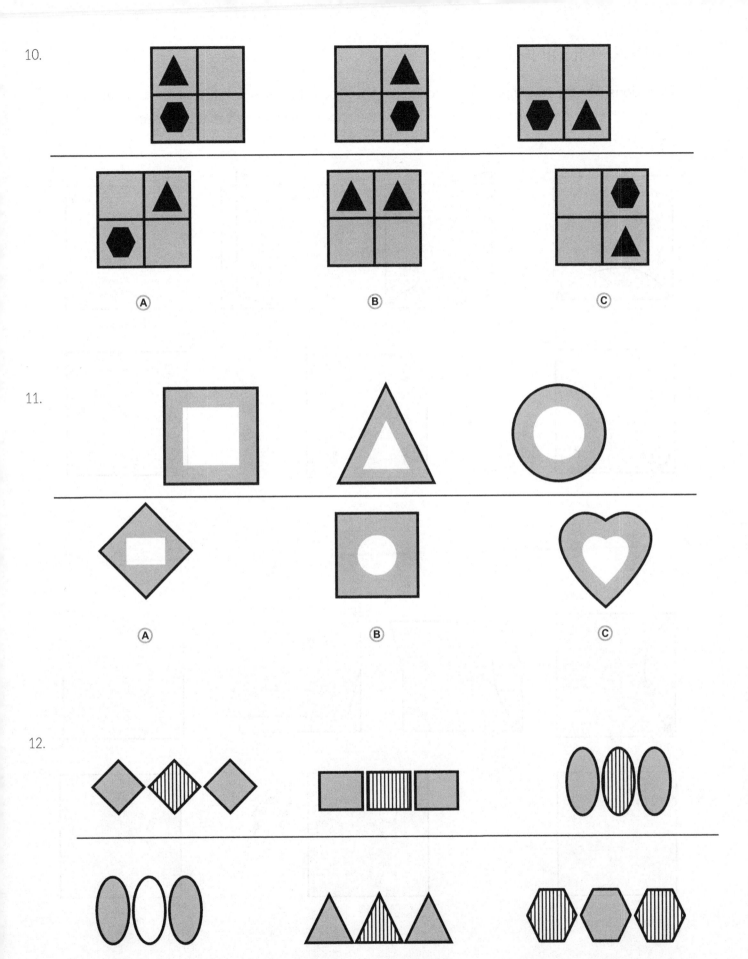

10.

A   B   C

11.

A   B   C

12.

A   B   C

PAPER FOLDING

Directions: The top row of pictures shows a sheet of paper. The paper was folded, then something was cut out. Which picture in the bottom row shows how the paper would look after its unfolded?

1.

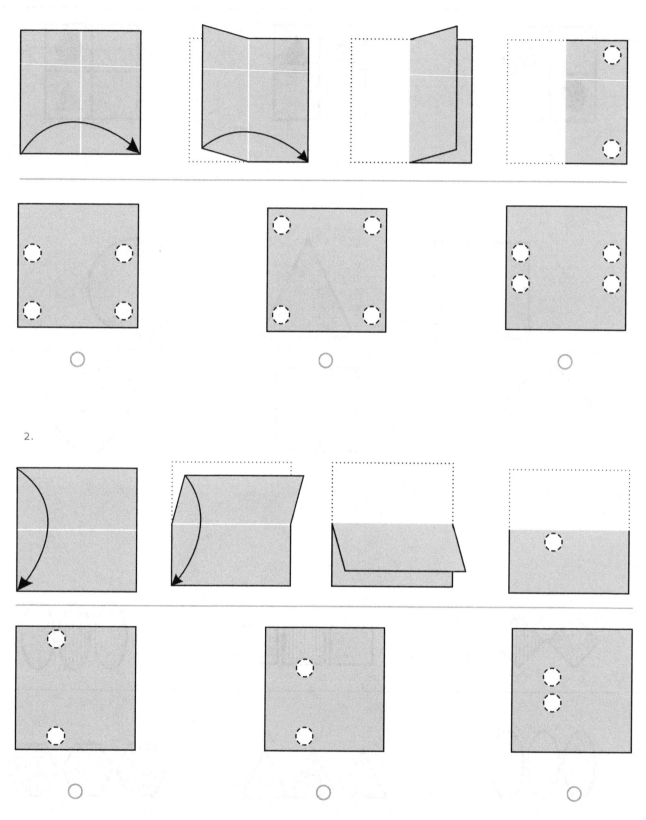

2.

3.

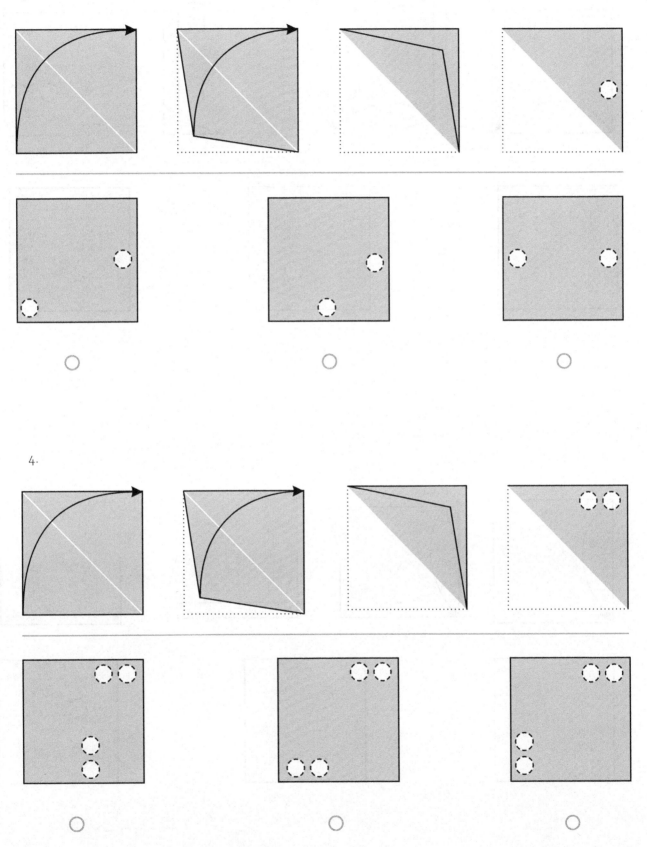

5.

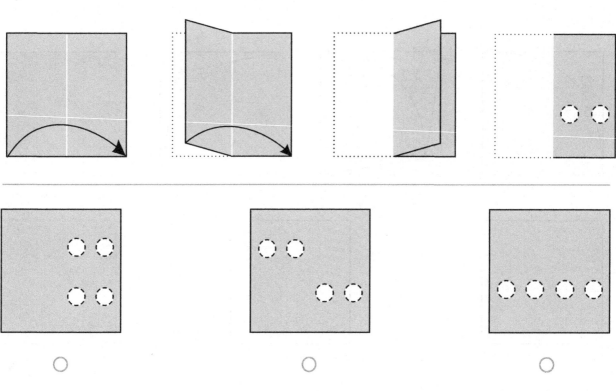

○   ○   ○

6.

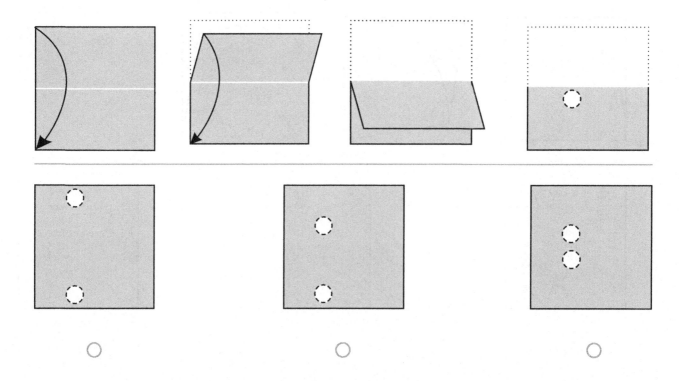

○   ○   ○

7.

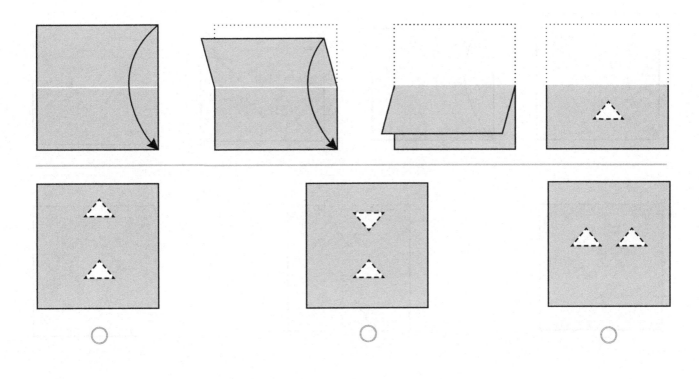

○   ○   ○

8.

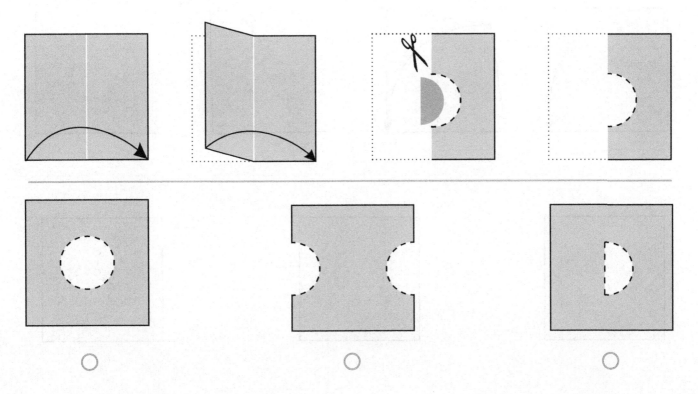

○   ○   ○

9.

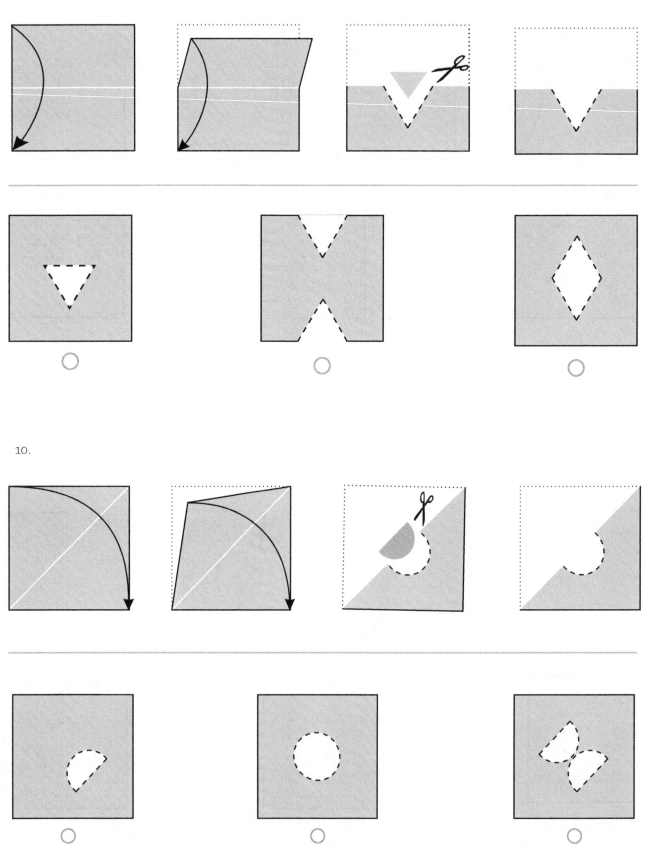

10.

NUMBER PUZZLES

Directions: Which train car should you choose so that the top train has the same number of items as the bottom train?

1.

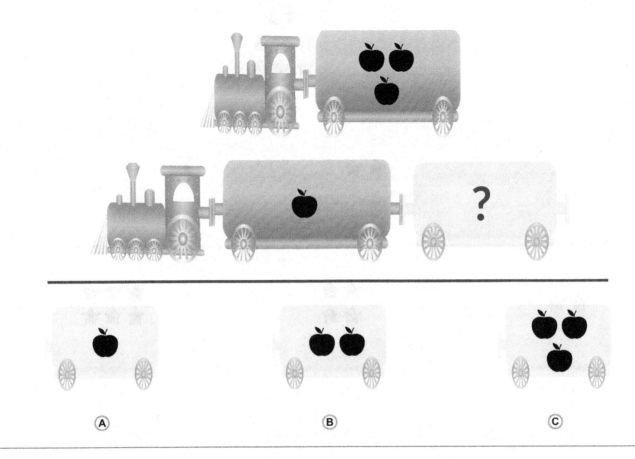

(A)   (B)   (C)

2.

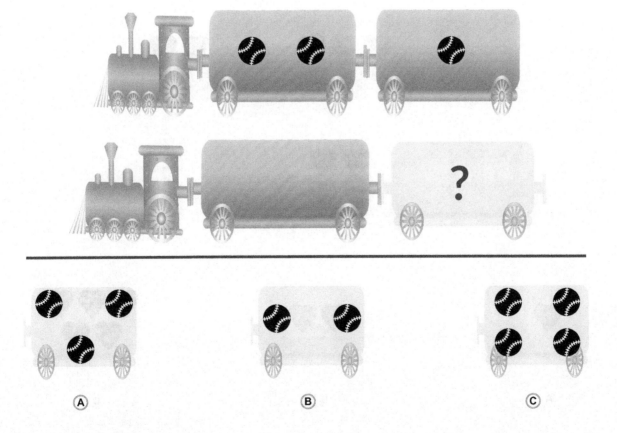

(A)   (B)   (C)

3.

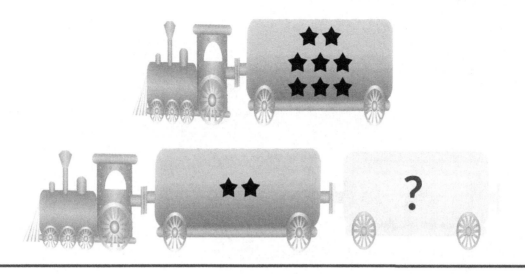

(A)   (B)   (C)

4.

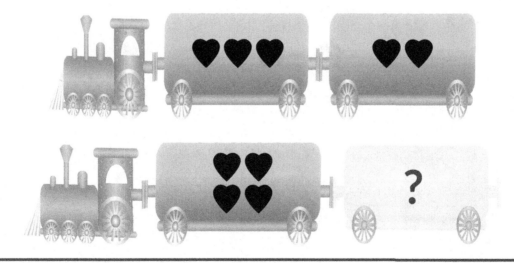

(A)   (B)   (C)

5.

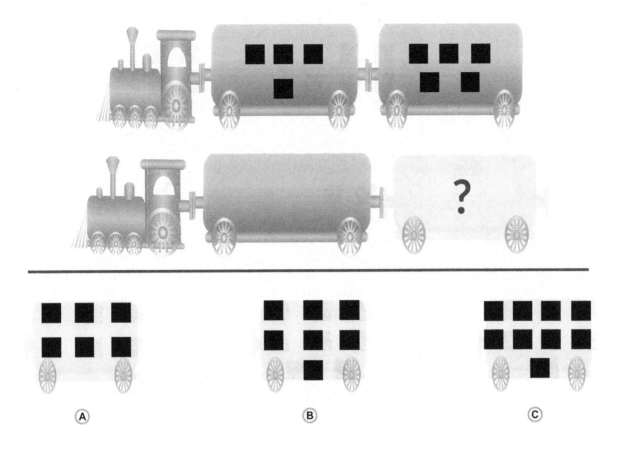

A B C

6.

A B C

95

7.

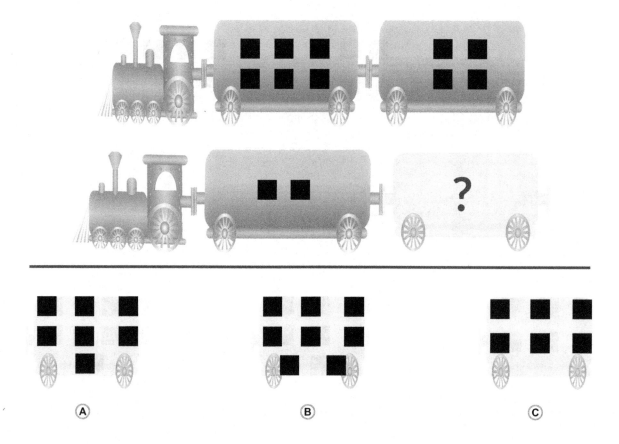

8.

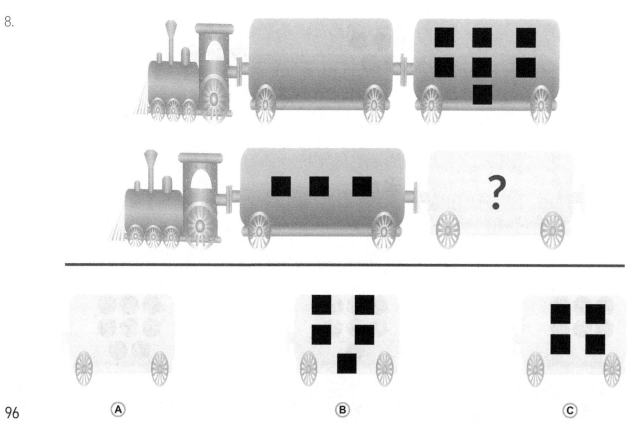

   A   B   C

9.

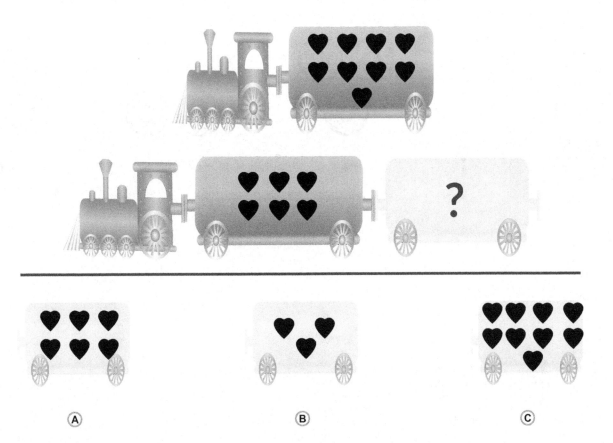

(A)	(B)	(C)

10.

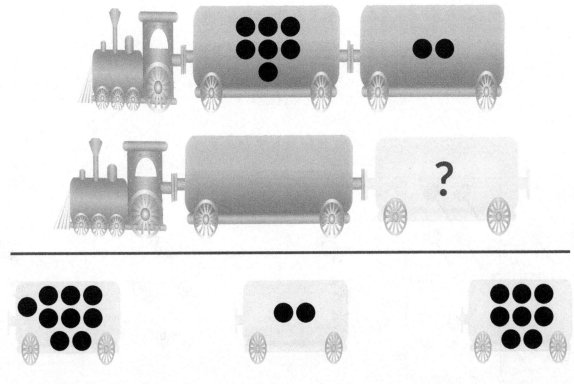

(A)	(B)	(C)

NUMBER ANALOGIES

Directions: The pictures on top go together in some way. One of the bottom boxes is empty. Which answer choice would make the bottom boxes go together like the top pictures do?

1.

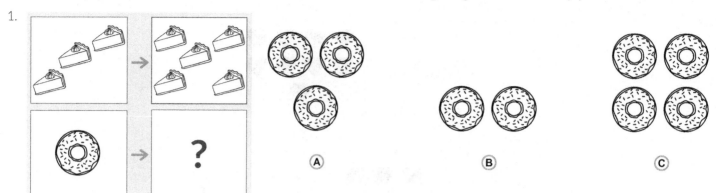

Ⓐ   Ⓑ   Ⓒ

2.

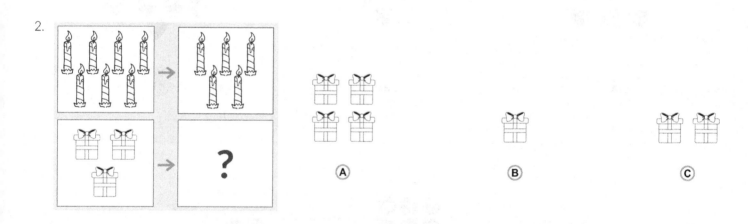

Ⓐ   Ⓑ   Ⓒ

3.

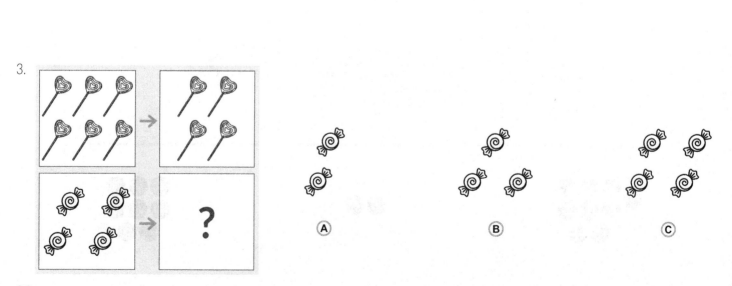

Ⓐ   Ⓑ   Ⓒ

4.

(A)

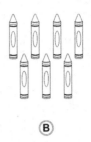

(B)

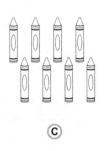

(C)

5.

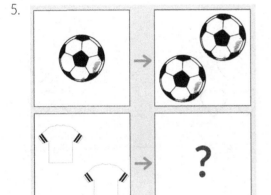

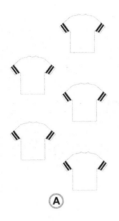

(A)

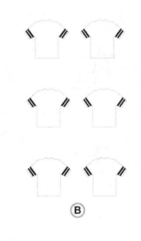

(B)

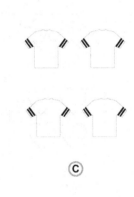

(C)

6.

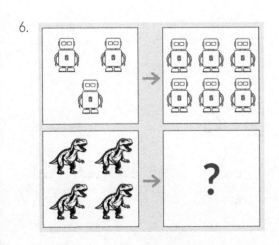

(A)

(B)

(C)

7.

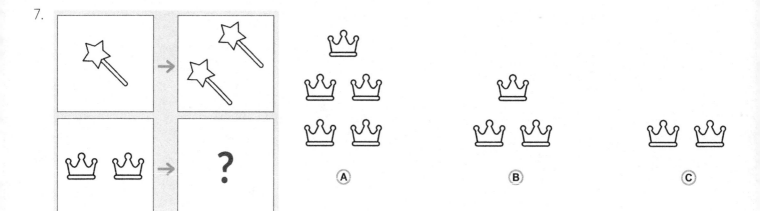

A   B   C

8.

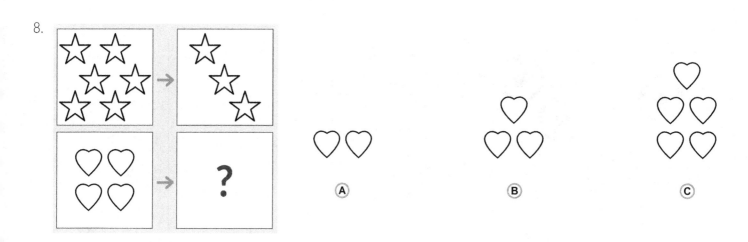

A   B   C

9.

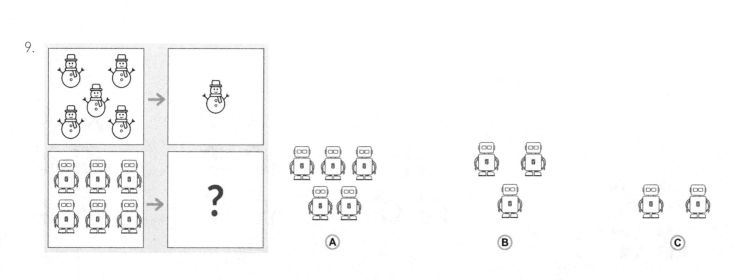

A   B   C

10.

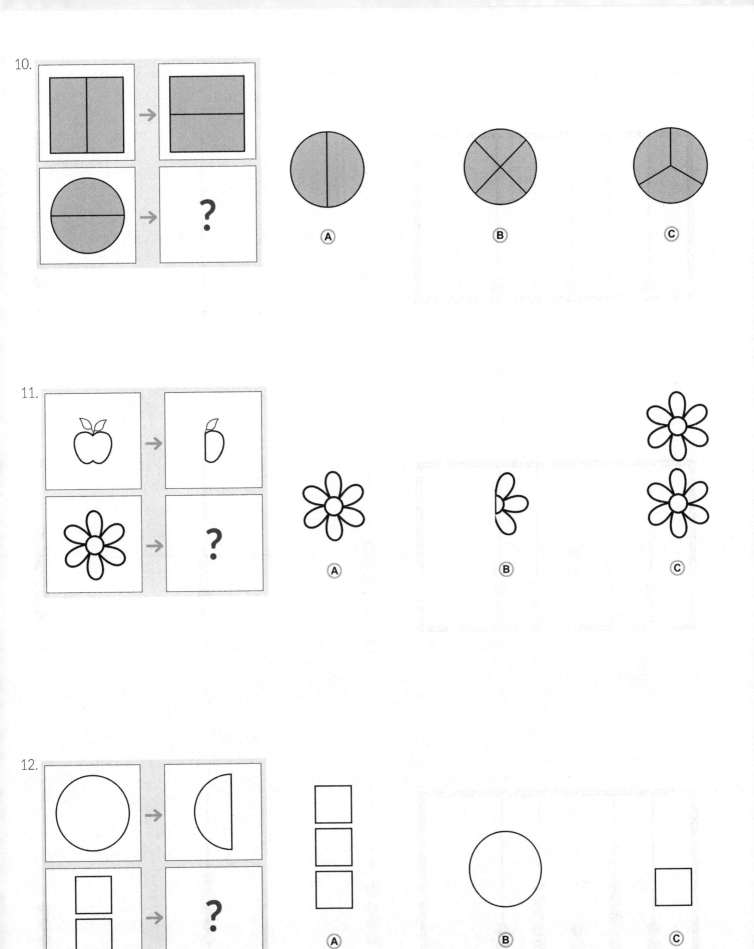

11.

12.

NUMBER SERIES

Directions: Which rod goes in the place of the missing rod to finish the pattern?

1.

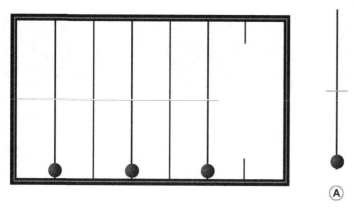

Ⓐ   Ⓑ   Ⓒ

2.

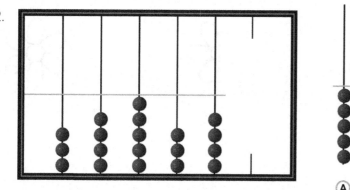

Ⓐ   Ⓑ   Ⓒ

3.

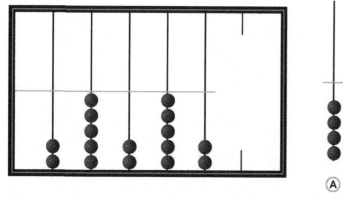

Ⓐ   Ⓑ   

Ⓒ

4.

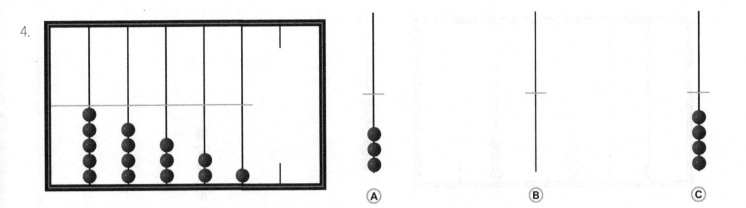

Ⓐ   Ⓑ   Ⓒ

5.

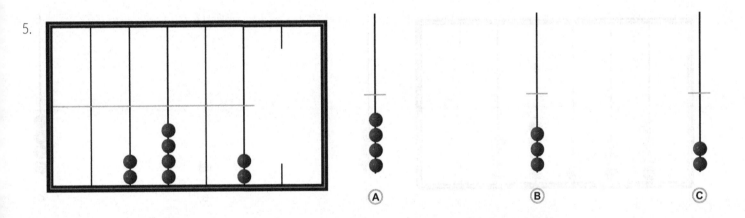

Ⓐ   Ⓑ   Ⓒ

6.

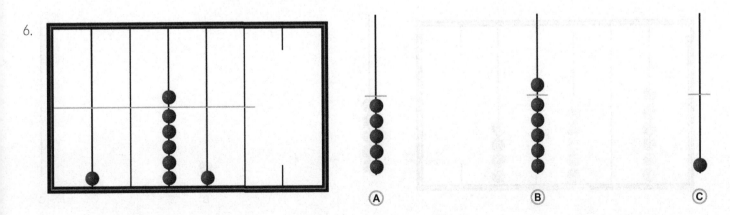

Ⓐ   Ⓑ   Ⓒ

7.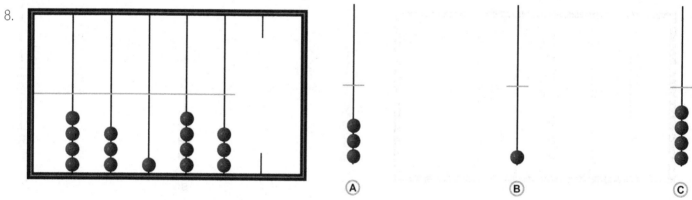

8.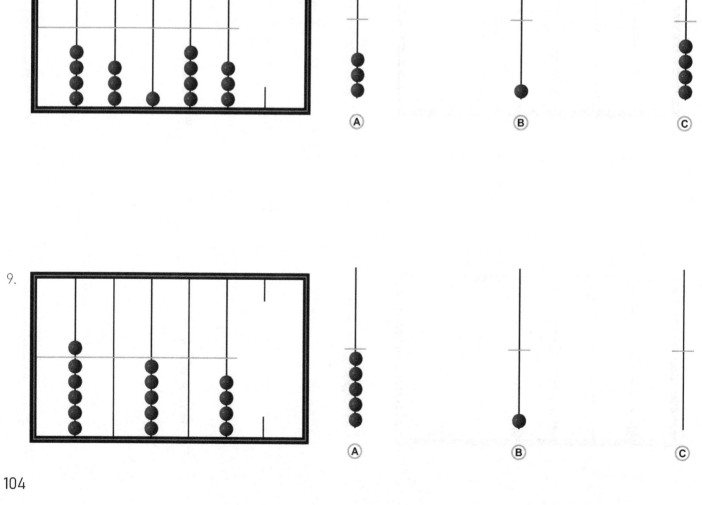

9.

10.

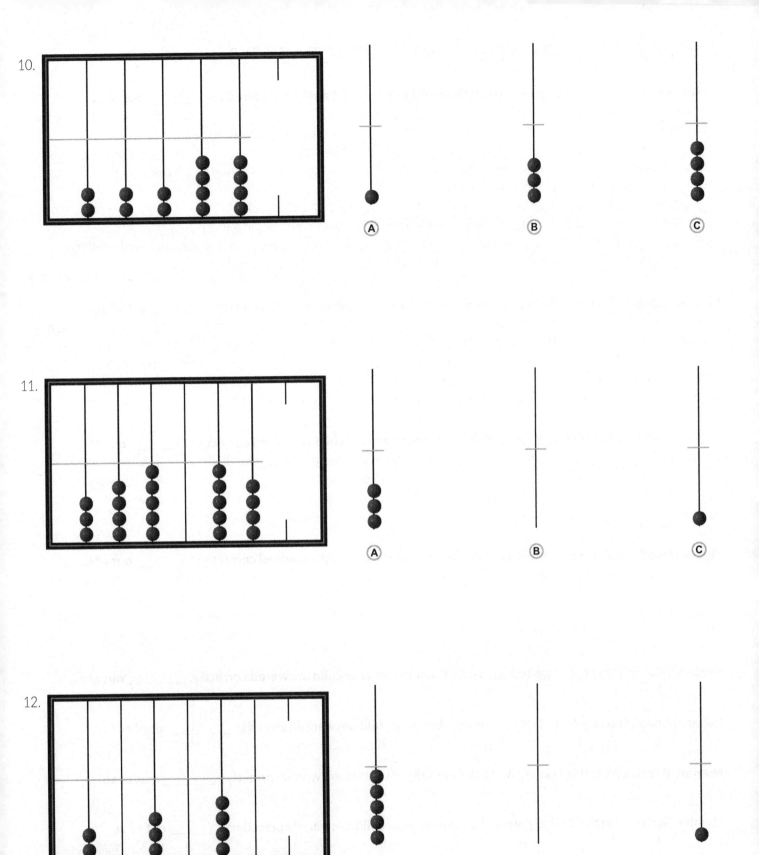

11.

12.

- END OF PRACTICE TEST 2 -

ANSWER KEY FOR KINDERGARTEN PRACTICE TEST 1

Picture Analogies (Practice Test 1) / Write the number your child answered correctly: _____ out of 14
1. B: animal > animal's home
2. C: food commonly eaten by animal > animal
3. A: adult version > baby version
4. B: opposites
5. A: similar animals (fish on top; flying insects on bottom)
6. C: many in a group > one
7. B: vehicle > item associated with vehicle
8. A: vehicle > where it travels
9. C: tool > worker who uses it (a hammer is used by a carpenter; a whisk and bowl are used by a baker/cook)
10. A: similar object (flowers on top; fruit on bottom)
11. B: product > creator (a painting is made by an artist; a pie is made by a baker/cook)
12. C: worker > vehicle used to do job (a farmer rides in a tractor; an astronaut rides in a spaceship)
13. B: drink or food > utensil used to consume (to drink a beverage you use a straw; to eat a steak you use a knife/fork)
14. A: animal > food that animal produces (a cow produces milk; a chicken produces eggs)

Figure Analogies (Practice Test 1) / Write the number your child answered correctly: _____ out of 14
1. A: a heart changes to a pentagon and vice versa
2. C: shape becomes gray
3. B: shape gets bigger
4. B: arrows on top point down; arrows on bottom face up
5. B: shape is filled with dots
6. A: one more shape
7. B: same shape
8. C: colors switch
9. C: flips
10. C: flips
11. A: gets bigger & turns gray
12. B: small shape moves to the right
13. A: bottom half turns gray
14. A: the inner shape & outer shape switch positions & sizes

Picture Classification (Practice Test 1) / Write the number your child answered correctly: _____ out of 14
1. B: sweet things
2. A: fruits
3. C: clothing worn on top half of your body
4. A: birds
5. A: boats
6. B: animal homes
7. C: round/spherical
8. A: body parts
9. B: plants
10. C: used for writing/drawing
11. B: sports equipment
12. A: drinks
13. B: slices
14. A: pairs

Figure Classification (Practice Test 1) / Write the number your child answered correctly: _____ out of 12
1. B: gray circles
2. B: filled with lines
3. B: gray
4. C: diamonds
5. A: circles
6. C: circles
7. A: triangles
8. C: small black diamond with larger white diamond
9. B: top half white & bottom half black
10. C: left half black & right half white
11. B: heart & star are either in the same row or same column
12. B: shape colors: black-white-black

Sentence Completion (Practice Test 1) / Write the number your child answered correctly: _____ out of 14
1. C   2. A   3. B   4. A   5. C   6. B   7. C   8. B   9. A   10. C   11. B   12. A   13. B   14. C

Paper Folding (Practice Test 1) / Write the number your child answered correctly: _____ out of 10
1. B   2. A   3. C   4. B   5. B   6. A   7. A   8. A   9. C   10. C

Number Puzzles (Practice Test 1) / Write the number your child answered correctly: _____ out of 10
1. C   2. B   3. C   4. C   5. A   6. B   7. B   8. A   9. B   10. C

Number Series (Practice Test 1) / Write the number your child answered correctly: _____ out of 14
1. C   2. A   3. B   4. C   5. A   6. B   7. B   8. B   9. A   10. C   11. A   12. B   13. A   14. C

Number Analogies (Practice Test 1) / Write the number your child answered correctly: _____ out of 12
1. C   2. B   3. A   4. B   5. B   6. C   7. B (double)   8. A (double)   9. B (half)   10. A
11. B (half)   12. C (half)

ANSWER KEY FOR KINDERGARTEN PRACTICE TEST 2

Picture Analogies (Practice Test 2) / Write the number your child answered correctly: _____ **out of 14**
1. B: similar object (shirts/hats)   2. A: body part > item worn on that body part (gloves on hands/glasses on eyes)
3. C: front > back
4. A: place where vehicle travels > vehicle (in the sky is where planes travel; in water is where canoes travel)
5. B: a nose is used to smell flowers; a mouth is used for drinks (like coffee)
6. C: object > container storing many of those objects   7. A: large > small
8. A: footprint > animal/person with that footprint   9. C: 1 > 2   10. A: person/animal > hand/paw
11. B: object from tree > tree that it comes from   12. B: open > closed   13. C: similar (instruments / writing tools)
14. A: food source > food (bread comes from wheat; milk comes from cows)

Picture Classification (Practice Test 2) / Write the number your child answered correctly: _____ **out of 14**
1. B: worn on feet   2. C: fish   3. A: bodies of water   4. C: tools   5. A: balls for sports
6. C: used for measuring 7. B: found in kitchens   8. A: tell time   9. B: vegetables
10. A: vehicles that travel on land   11. C: furniture
12. A: where people can live (house, cabin, teepee, apartments)   13. A: cube-shaped   14. C: vehicles traveling in air

Sentence Completion (Practice Test 2) / Write the number your child answered correctly: _____ **out of 14**
1. A   2. C   3. C   4. A   5. B   6. C   7. B   8. C   9. A   10. C   11. A   12. C   13. B   14. A

Figure Analogies (Practice Test 2) / Write the number your child answered correctly: _____ **out of 14**
1. A: 1 is added   2. C: a circle changes to a parallelogram & vice versa   3. B: shape fills with lines   4. C: same
5. A: triangles point same direction   6. C: smaller white shape is added   7. B: flips
8. A: gets bigger & turns black   9. C: shape moves to opposite side   10. B: top half fills with dots
11. C: shapes switch colors   12. A: shape order reverses
13. B: shape position & size switches   14. A: shape position & size switches

Figure Classification (Practice Test 2) / Write the number your child answered correctly: _____ **out of 12**
1. C: filled with vertical lines   2. C: line inside circle is diagonal from upper left to lower right
3. A: gray heart on left & white heart on right   4. B: rectangles   5. B: 3 gray/1 white
6. C: larger black shape & smaller solid gray shape
7. B: larger gray shape & smaller black shape; shapes are the same
8. A: rectangles cut in half   9. C: shape halves
10. C: hexagon & triangle inside the same half of the square
11. C: smaller white shape & larger gray shape; shapes are the same
12. B: group of 3 shapes: gray-filled with lines-gray

Paper Folding (Practice Test 2) / Write the number your child answered correctly: _____ **out of 10**
1. B   2. C   3. B   4. C   5. C   6. C   7. B   8. A   9. C   10. B

Number Puzzles (Practice Test 2) / Write the number your child answered correctly: _____ **out of 10**
1. B   2. A   3. C   4. A   5. C   6. A   7. B   8. C   9. B   10. A

Number Analogies (Practice Test 2) / Write the number your child answered correctly: _____ **out of 12**
1. A   2. B   3. A   4. C   5. C (double)   6. C   7. B   8. A (half)   9. C   10. A (shapes divided in half)
11. B   12. C (half)

Number Series (Practice Test 2) / Write the number your child answered correctly: _____ **out of 12**
1. B   2. A   3. B   4. B   5. A   6. B   7. C   8. B   9. C   10. C   11. A   12. A

Check out our other Savant Prep™ books!

Available on Amazon®

WAY TO GO!

Congrats to:

_____

write name here

Thanks for your help and hard work!

Made in the USA
Columbia, SC
04 February 2024

31444734R00063